LEXICON OF
OIL & VINEGAR
Origin • Taste • Use • Recipes

Anne Iburg

REBO
PUBLISHERS

All information in this book has been provided to the best knowledge of the author and has been tested by her as well as the publishers with the greatest possible care. It can nevertheless not be assumed that all mistakes are completely excluded. By supplying this information, the author does not assume any responsibility nor does the author provide any form of guarantee. Neither party is responsible for any possible incorrect information supplied in the text.

© 2004 Rebo International b.v., Lisse, The Netherlands

Text: Anne Iburg
Typesetting: AdAm Studio, Prague, The Czech Republic
Cover design: AdAm Studio, Prague, The Czech Republic

Translation: Helena Hurtová for Agentura Abandon, Prague, The Czech Republic
Proofreading: Emily Sands, Eva Munk, Jeff Rubinoff

ISBN 90 366 1693 X

Contents

10   **Introduction**

14   **Vinegar**

16   History of vinegar

22   What exactly is vinegar?

24   Production of vinegar

30   Vinegar & Health

36   Vinegar & Beauty

40   Vinegar ingredients

42   Vinegar in the household

46   How to make vinegar

52   Vinegar from A to Z

52   *Aceto Balsamico*

62   *Wine vinegar*

70   *Malt vinegar*

76   *Distilled vinegar*

82   *Champagne vinegar*

90   *Sherry vinegar*

96   *Herbal and spiced vinegars*

102   *Apple cider vinegar*

110   *Fruit vinegar*

114	*Vegetable vinegar*
118	*Rice vinegar*
124	*Rasin vinegar*
130	*Whey vinegar*
134	What is each type of vinegar suitable for?

136   **Cooking Oil**

138	History of Cooking Oil
144	Production of Cooking Oil
150	Cooking Oil Ingredients
155	Cooking Oil & Health
159	Cooking Oil & External use
162	Cooking Oil in the Household
166	How to Flavor Cooking Oil
170	Cooking Oil from A to Z
170	*Peanut oil*
175	*Hazelnut oil*
182	*Macadamia nut oil*
188	*Walnut oil*
194	*Almond oil*
200	*Olive oil*
216	*Palm oil*
220	*Soybean oil*
226	*Sunflower oil*
232	*Linseed oil*

238   *Corn oil*

244   *Wheatgerm oil*

250   *Poppyseed oil*

256   *Sesame oil*

262   *Canola oil*

268   *Safflower seed oil*

274   *Pumpkinseed oil*

280   *Grapeseed oil*

286   *Special vegetable oils*

290   What is each type of cooking oil suitable for?

292   Index

296   Recipes

298   List of illustrations

All recipes are for 4 people unless otherwise noted.

Introduction

OIL AND VINEGAR – AN IDEAL COUPLE

Oil and vinegar have been essential parts of our culinary traditions for thousands of years. In the 20th century, they lost their positive image. People were persuaded to think that: "Vinegar tastes sour," and "Oil is fattening." Both ideas have been taken out of context. Vinegar's tangy taste and complex flawors create an interesting sourness. Moreover, daily consumption of a reasonable amount of oil does not lead to serious weight gain.

Oil and vinegar confidently challenge their negative image. More and more people are realising that both oil and vinegar are vital and nourishing components of food. The variety of oils and vinegars has increased enormously over the last few years. Oil and vinegar complement each other very well. The best example is salad, which many people prefer to eat with oil and vinegar.

Good combinations include olive oil and Aceto Balsamico or walnut oil and sherry vinegar. Alternatively, a prime cut of meat can be cooked with high quality sunflower oil and the undesirable, charred bits can be removed with fine herb vinegar. This lexicon offers many traditional and modern ways to use oil and vinegar, alone or in combination. It may surprise you!

VINEGAR – EVERYONE'S FAD

Vinegar has become a fad in the last few years. Someone who wants to be recognized for their cooking does not use low-quality vinegar. It must be Aceto Balsamico, sherry vinegar or a quality wine vinegar. Vinegar is not only good in salads, but a gourmet can taste it in sauces made by the best cooks. The latest thing in distinguished dining is drinkable vinegar, offered as an aperitif instead of sherry, champagne or liqueurs like fruit brandy or aquavit.

Whether you follow food fashion or not, while standing in front of the vinegar shelf in a typical supermarket, you will find that the choice is vast. So you have to decide which type of vinegar is the right one for you. The lexicon will help you make the best decision.

OIL – MORE THAN JUST FAT

While sunflower-seed oil, olive oil, thistle seed oil and polyunsaturated fatty acids were prevalent in the 1980s, rapeseed and soy oils now tend to dominate the health food market. What makes oils different from each other? How are oils produced and why are there differences even within one type of oil? You will find detailed and knowledgeable answers to all of your questions in this lexicon.

REFERENCES TO THE LEXICON

The following points of reference will help you quickly familiarize yourself with the *Oil & Vinegar Lexicon*:

The book is divided into sections on *"Vinegar"* and *"Oil"*. Each section has the same layout. We start with general information about the historical significance of the oil or vinegar, different production processes, the various uses and ingredients and its importance for health. Short descriptions will present the special characteristics of each oil or vinegar. You will get to know different varieties, their ingredients and what foods to cook with them. In addition, each entry contains at least two recipes to help you enjoy the various tastes of the oils and vinegars.

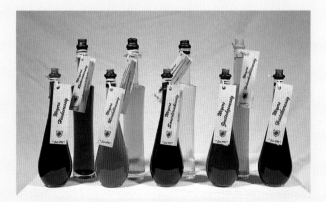

Vinegar

History of vinegar

VINEGAR IS OLDER THAN HOMO SAPIENS

Man did not invent vinegar; he discovered it. Our ancestors had only to decide whether and how to use it.

Vinegar forms naturally: if ethanol is thoroughly dissolved in water, the acetic acid bacteria oxidize ethanol and turn it into vinegar. Since acetic acid bacteria are primitive life forms, they appear in the evolutionary record long before the arrival of mankind. Carbon oxidation is one of the most basic processes in the history of evolution and thus vinegar existed before the beginning of human history.

HOW MAN DISCOVERED VINEGAR

Nobody can say precisely who discovered vinegar. From a historical standpoint, people have known about the production of alcohol and vinegar for about 10,000 years. The oldest evidence was found in the Middle East. You can read in the Talmud that a large amount of wine turned to vinegar while the Jewish people were transporting it to the Promised Land from Mesopotamia. Babylonians used vinegar for food conservation as early as 5,000 BC. In any case, vinegar was not made in ancient Babylon with wine and beer, but with the juice of date palms or date honey. The traditional process of making vinegar from wine and beer became generally accepted before the Classical period. The Phoenicians traditionally made vinegar from apples or apple-juice.

Vinegar as a kosher food

The Old Testament offers plenty of evidence that people knew about the production and use of vinegar before Christ's birth. There is evidence that in Palestine during the 7th century BC, wine was left to ferment in large, wine-producing centers. It is certain that an exact understanding of the process was not available at that time. However, vinegar was an important seasoning and it was also diluted like wine for drinking. People began to use it as a preservative and a vinegar trade may have developed in the Mediterranean area. We can safety assume that unexpected amounts of vinegar resulted from a lack of familiarity with wine conservation processes. It would not have been difficult for people at that time to use up the vinegar because the consumption of vinegar was much higher than it is today.

Vinegar in the Classical Period

Wine production was widespread in Ancient Egypt, Greece and the Roman Empire. People also knew how to produce vinegar. In the Classical period, vinegar was stored and transported in amphorae.

A work called *De agricultura* by the Roman Cato is one of the few preserved documents verifying the use of vinegar. If you have mastered Latin, you can read, for example, that slaves were given a mixture of wine, vinegar and boiled water. The higher a Roman stood in society, the better quality of drink he was able to consume. A mixture made of eggs, vinegar and water was a favorite drink among Roman soldiers.

Vinegar in the Middle Ages

After the decline of the Roman Empire, only homemade vinegar was available in Europe until the early Middle Ages. There was no vinegar trade. In the 14th century, while guilds were being founded and industry was budding, the vinegar trade developed in the area around Orleans on the Loire River. Vinegar was made from beer and wine mash, half of which is composed of sediments. The basic ingredients were put into open, wooden barrels and left in the open air. Acetic acid bacteria could multiply in the standing liquid, which resulted in oxidized alcohol.

In the Middle Ages, vinegar was a valuable drink. This is recorded in the epic, *Vita Mathilidis*, written by a Benedictine monk named Donizo von Canossa. It describes how the king, and later emperor, Heinrich von Bonifatius von Canossa IV, demanded a particular type of vinegar. According to the Italians it was Balsamico. The term 'Balsamico' was first recorded in the middle of the 18th century in a letter from Antonio Boccolari.

In the Middle Ages, vinegar was not only used as a preservative, a seasoning and a drink. It was also considered to have healing powers. When the plague was raging in Europe, people rubbed themselves with vinegar when exchanging goods and money to prevent infection.

ACETIC ACIDS DISCOVERED BY SCIENTISTS

Although people wanted to produce vinegar industrially for a long time, they did not know exactly what processes were taking place. The exact processes were first explained by scientists in the modern age.

In 1793, the well-known chemist, Antoine Laurent de Lavoisier, announced for the first time that acetic acid production might be an oxidation process. Friedrich Traugott Kützing, a druggist and botanist, propounded a thesis for 50 years suggesting that microbes were responsible for the formation of vinegar. In 1862, Louis

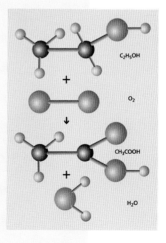

C_2H_5OH

+

O_2

↓

CH_3COOH

+

H_2O

Pasteur confirmed Kützing's theory by discovering the microbes.

VINEGAR – PRECURSOR OF SODA

In the 19th century, vinegar diluted with water was a favorite thirst-quenching drink in the summer time. The acidic water was refined with a pinch of natron (a type of baking soda). The vinegar reacted to force the carbonic acid out of the natron, producing a refreshing fizzy drink.

THE VINEGAR INDUSTRY IN GERMANY

The vinegar industry can be illustrated by the story of the Kühne Company. The enterprise was a typical vinegar-

producing business. In 1722, Johann Daniel Epinius opened a vinegar factory in Berlin. His widow sold the business 39 years later to Daniel Friedrich Teichert, Friedrich Wilhelm Kühne's brother-in-law. Two generations later, his cousin, Carl Ernst Wilhelm Kühne, took over the vinegar factory and gave his name to the business. After a fast vinegar-producing process was invented by Schüzenbach, the business transformed from a small family enterprise into an industrial producer in 1832. In 1876, the company was chosen as the royal vinegar supplier. While the range of products was expanding, the enormous growth and success of the business continued through the turn of the century. In 1905, Kühne introduced bottled vinegar to the market under the brand name Surol. Vinegar had previously been sold in jugs or barrels.

What exactly is vinegar?

Vinegar is the focus of The Regulation of the Vinegar and Acetic Substances Trade and is defined as a product containing at least ½ oz, but no more than 1 ½ oz, of acetic acid per ½ cup. Vinegar is basically made with alcohol and acetic acid fermentation. The proportion of remaining alcohol in vinegar – except wine vinegar – must not exceed 0.5% of the volume. This was agreed upon in the standard adopted in August 2000 and it is valid for all EU countries.

Common varieties of vinegar contain between 5 and 6% acetic acid.

They can be divided into three groups:

The term *vinegar* refers to vinegar produced by an organic process, whereas acetic acid vinegar and vinegar produced with acetic substances are products containing synthetically produced acetic acids diluted with water or mixtures of natural vinegar and

THE DEFINITION OF AN ACETIC SUBSTANCE

An acetic substance is an acetic acid that has been diluted with water and that contains more than ½ oz but not more than 1 oz of acetic acid in 3 oz. If the amount of acetic acid in vinegar is more than 11%, the following instructions must be included on the package: "Attention! Do not use undiluted!"

chemically produced acetic acids. The latter varieties do not contain flavored ingredients at all. They simply taste sour. That is why it is worth trying different types of naturally produced vinegar.

VINEGAR PRODUCTION PROCESSES

The organic fermentation process is classified as an anaerobic reaction (where oxygen does not play a role) resulting in acquired energy. The energy formed manifests itself in the form of heat energy. The process is named after the final product formed during the process. Thus, alcohol is produced by alcoholic fermentation, lactic acid is produced during lactic acid fermentation and acetic acid is produced during acetic acid fermentation. However, this definition of the fermentation of acetic acid is not completely correct because an aerobic process only takes place if oxygen is present. In principle, alcohol fermentation must precede the fermentation of acetic acid. During fermentation, sugar is combined with alcohol and carbon dioxide and the alcohol formed during the process turns into acetic acid. During alcohol fermentation, yeast facilitates the sugar reaction. During acetic acid fermentation, bacteria, called acetic acid bacteria, promote the alcohol reaction.

Alcohol fermentation:
$C_6H_{12}O_6 \rightarrow 2\ C_2H_5OH + 2\ CO_2$

Acetic acid fermentation:
$C_2H_5OH + O_2 \rightarrow CH_3COOH + H_2O$

Production of vinegar

VINEGAR PRODUCTION

The production process of vinegar today is basically the same as it was thousands of years ago, although the technology has changed tremendously. In principle, vinegar production can be divided into three categories: the surface method, the generator or the bound method and the acetate or submersible process.

The oldest process is the surface method, on the basis of which vinegar has been produced for market since the Middle Ages. The oldest commercial vinegar production process was named after a French town on the Loire River. The Orleans process uses wine or another alcohol solution, such as beer or a high quality sparkling wine or champagne, as its main ingredient. The liquid is stored in wooden barrels that hold between 53 and 80 gallons. The barrels are filled half-full or a third full with a mixture of wine and wine vinegar, or with a similar basic ingredient. Above the surface of the liquid there are holes in the barrel so that the acetic acid bacteria are thoroughly supplied with oxygen from the air. The bacteria form a slippery skin on the surface known as the vinegar mother or the comb skin. After oxodization, the vinegar producer can draw off 3 to 4 gallons of raw vinegar and replace

it with wine. The acetic acid bacteria are active unless the alcohol content falls to 1%. At this point, all of the vinegar is carefully drained off so that the vinegar mother is not disturbed.

The same barrel can than be filled with wine and wine vinegar mash. The process continues until there is a tremendous amount of pulp in the vinegar and a proper cleaning of the barrel is necessary.

Vinegar is still made using this method. Only a few innovations have been made, such as propping up the skin of bacteria with a set of small, wooden sticks.

At the beginning of the 18th century, the surface process was improved with the development of the Boerhave method. Unlike the Orleans process, the liquid is set in motion so that the acid mash fermentation is faster.

The bound method was introduced in 1815 by Schuezenbach and therefore it is also sometimes called the Schuezenbach process, or the fast acetic method, or the German method. In the bound method, the acetic acid bacteria are bound to a filtering substrate. Originally, beech chips with rough surfaces were used as substrates. There are acetic acid bacteria on these chips. Other supporting materials include wooden stakes, corn stalks or grapevines. The chips are then preserved and put in wooden barrels with holes on the bottom so that the air can get to the mash. The mash is poured from the pot onto the chips and seeps through slowly to the bottom. The time limit must be determined so that the vinegar has time to form and flow down. If the mash only consists of water and pure alcohol, the saturated chips can be used for 30 to 50 years. With vinegar, the useful life of the chips is much shorter.

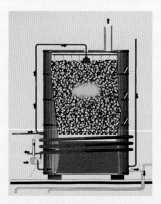

Other improved variations of the Schuezenbach method include the generator method and the Fring method. The vinegar is pumped and transferred from the bottom to the top and passes over the substrate again so that it can achieve a higher acidic content. Unlike the original Schuezenbach method, the mash flows over the substrate repeatedly.

The most modern and efficient type of vinegar production is the submersible process, also known as the acetate method. The remarkable innovation is that acetic acid bacteria float freely in the liquid and are able to multiply they do not have to float on the surface or be bound to the supporting material. Copolymerized vinegars containing highly concentrated acetic acid bacteria are added to the basic ingredients. The production of acetic acid is completed within hours, not days or weeks as is typical of other methods. The oxygen is forced into the liquid. When acetic acid bacteria have produced acetic acid to 0.3% of the volume of the mash, a third of the tank content is replaced with fresh mash. The acidic content of raw vinegars made this way can be as high as 15%. Acetate tanks hold as much as 53 to 13,1209 gallons. In the latter case, it is possible to produce 3,170 gallons of raw vinegar a day. Using the submersible process, you can make every possible variety of vinegar, from fruit to malt.

THE REPROCESSING OF SYNTHETIC VINEGAR

After fermentation, raw vinegar contains pulp. This is removed from the vinegar during filtration. The vinegar is then stored in a cool, dark place without oxygen. As soon as oxygen gets into the vinegar, the acetic acid bacteria resume the oxidation process. In any case, if oxidation is prevented, acetic acid bacteria die out and ultimately become inactive. To make absolutely sure that there is no oxygen left, raw vinegar is stored at higher concentrations of nitrogen and carbon dioxide.

Pure varieties of vinegar, particularly those produced by the bound method, are sometimes aged. During this time, the vinegar will develop its flavor. At the same time, pulp containing impurities accumulates at the bottom.

If this process is inadequate to purify the vinegar, it can be fined like wine. Fining is the process in which the vinegar is improved by adding certain ingredients with

different characteristics. Such ingredients can include bentonite, gelatin or silicate. The acidic content, set by law, may need to be modified so that the vinegar has an acidic content of anywhere from 5 to 8%. Then the vinegar is filtered and sterilized. Sterilization is rarely done cold and is usually accomplished by pasteurization.

The most common varieties of vinegar are pasteurized, during which process the remaining proteins in the vinegar are denatured. This process guarantees that the remaining acetic acid bacteria are finally inactive and that the vinegar is free of foreign germs. Vinegars that have been filtered and sterilized cold can still contain acetic acid bacteria. The filtering must be sufficiently effective that the acetic acid bacteria cannot become active again.

Vinegar & Health

These days, questions are often asked about the health benefits of food products. You can find many different opinions on the topic in literature. Vinegar was considered a medication as early as the Classical period. Hildegard von Bingen also attributed a healing effect to vinegar. There are also alternative methods of nutrition, such as the combined diet and acid-base diets, which suggest that vinegar is responsible for the hyperacidity of the body.

VINEGAR ... FROM THE HUMAN BODY?

Although not exactly vinegar, the human body involuntarily makes 1½ to1 ½ oz of acetic acid every day. This will depend on the energy level of the individual. The higher the energy level, the more acetic acid is produced because it is a product of the breakdown of the major nutrients, carbohydrates and fat. It is then futher broken down into carbohydrates and water. The carbon dioxide is exhaled through the bronchial tubes and the water is excreted out of the body through urine and defecation as well as through sweating and breathing. The consumption of 3 oz of vinegar means that the body's metabolism must break down approximately 0.17 to 0.22 extra ounces of acetic acid. In any case, this amount will not throw someone's metabolism off-balance.

VINEGAR AS A MEDICINE IN THE CLASSICAL PERIOD

Vinegar was considered a medicine by the Egyptians, and later by the Romans. In ancient Greece, vinegar was prescribed by Hippocrates (460–370 BC) and other healers for internal and external protection against many diseases. In his textbook, *Corpus Hippocraticum*, Hippocrates also described the healing effects of vinegar. Hippocrates's family, the Asclepiads, were said to be related to the demigod Asklepios, Apollo's son and a god of healing in ancient Greece. According to family tradition, Hippocrates' father taught his son about the effects and use of vinegar when he was still a child. In his journeys through Asia Minor and Greece, he put his medical skills to use as a wandering doctor. Famous and respected everywhere, he returned to the island of Kos to practice, write and teach medicine at his own school.

WARNING:

More concentrated acetic acid, with more than 0.4 oz per ½ cup, causes burning of the mucous membrane of the oral cavity and throat as well as of the digestive tract. The lining of the mouth is more sensitive than the skin on the exterior. You may have noticed that when acetic substances come into contact with skin, they burn. If concentrated acetic acid touches the lining of your mouth, the pain can be excruciating.

First aid: Immediately drink a large amount of liquid, preferably water or buttermilk, and seek medical help.

Vinegar in medicine during the Middle Ages

During the Middle Ages, health was primarily the domain of the monasteries. Vinegar was regarded by the clergy as a medication. At the time of the Plague, people even believed that rubbing vinegar into the body would ward off infection. The abbess Hildegard von Bingen (1098–1179), a contemporary of Barbarossa, wrote: "Vinegar goes with every meal, and when it is added to dishes of similar taste, so that it does not take on its own flavor, you will hardly notice the vinegar. When consuming it with food, it cleanses the body by reducing the amount of fluid, and helps the body to digest the food well. But if too much vinegar is added to dishes, so that the taste of the dish is overwhelmed by the flavor, it can do harm to the eater."

VINEGAR IN MODERN MEDICINE

You can still buy vinegar in drugstores. In Europe, it certainly remains a drugstore standard. Nor has it lost its importance as a medication in Asia. The first modern doctors prescribed vinegar for internal and external use. Vinegar packs relieve swelling and stimulate digestion. People were woken from narcosis with concentrated vinegar. In the 18th and 19th centuries, a small open bottle of vinegar was put on the night table for clearing the air in the sick rooms. However, modern medicine doubted vinegar's effecialy and vinegar is not much used in modern medicine. All the same, it still has a place in medicine cabinets.

VINEGAR: A MODERN MEDICATION

At present, vinegar is usually used only for minor illnesses, such as contusions and colds, but you may hear it recommended as a wonder drug for all kinds of complaints. Dont expect too much! Miracles are seldom seen and vinegar cannot solve every health problem. However, you can find out here what positive influences vinegar can have on your health.

VINEGAR STIMULATES DIGESTION: a dose of vinegar taken with indigestible dishes, such as lentil or pea soup, reduces flatulence. There is a theory that says that acetic acid and stomach acid have a special chemistry when combined, that aids in the release of particular nutrients. In the small intestine, nutrients are absorbed more easily, so less food passes to the large intestine to be broken down by the gut bacteria. During this process, waste gases are formed and released through the anus as flatulence. The production of gases is therefore reduced and flatulence is prevented when acetic acid is taken.

You can clean the oral cavity and throat by gargling with acetic water (1 spoonful of vinegar stirred into 1 glass of water). Afterwards, nothing should be eaten because everything you ingest diminishes the cleansing effect. Gargling should be done alongside brushing your teeth and the effects are comparable. Regular gargling with acetic water cleans the oral cavity, disinfects the mouth and stimulates salivation, a natural protection against infection.

Rubbing vinegar into the skin helps to ward off mosquitoes, wasps and bees. The itching and swelling of a mosquito bite can be relieved by rubbing vinegar on it. As the vinegar cools and disinfects the skin, the swelling around the bite is reduced and the itching is temporarily abated. Put some vinegar on a cotton pad and rub the mosquito bite again for heightened effectiveness.

Vinegar & Beauty

You find yourself in the best company if you apply vinegar as a cosmetic. The beautiful and famous queen of Egypt, Cleopatra, was also familiar with the beautifying effects of vinegar.

VINEGAR CLEANSES THE COMPLEXION

Vinegar has a light exfoliating effect on a mixed (oily and dry in patches) complexion and can rid the skin of excess oil. There are different options for using vinegar as a cosmetic.

FACE WASHING: put 1 spoonful of vinegar into ½ cup water. Close your eyes and wash your face with your hands or with a washcloth. If the solution gets in your eyes, rinse with water immediately.

LOTION: You can use diluted vinegar mixed with water in a ratio of 1:1. Always wash your face first and then soak a cotton or gauze pad in the appropriate dilution. Apply lightly to dirty and oily problem spots on the forehead or chin. After the application of the vinegar, apply a moisturizing cream. Please use vinegar with care as with any beauty product.

FACIAL STEAM: warm up a mixture of vinegar and water in a ratio of 1:1 in a pot until the liquid starts to steam a little. It should not boil. Pour the mixture in a bowl. Place your face above it and put a large bath towel over both your head and the bowl so that the heat does not escape.

Close your eyes and inhale the rising vapor through your nose. You will breathe more freely and your skin will be softer and dead skin cells, grease, and wax can be removed easier. Afterwards, your skin will be clearer and the acidic vinegar will have a disinfecting effect.

MASQUE: a facial pack with vinegar also has a cleansing and disinfecting effect. Mix half a cup of healing mud with approximately 4 to 5 tablespoontuls of vinegar. Apply the paste thickly to clean skin, avoiding the area around the eyes. After 20 to 30 minutes, thoroughly rinse away the dry masque with lukewarm water.

ATTENTION:
It is not wise to use vinegar if you have extremely dry or sensitive skin. If your skin becomes tight or red, you should not use products containing vinegar.

VINEGAR REFRESHES THE BODY

Vinegar was regarded as the soda of the poor for a long time. But it is also used externally to refresh and keep the body fit.

BATH: A vinegar bath is refreshing for the whole body. Run the tub full of pleasantly warm water. Add 2 cups of fine vinegar, (apple vinegar, for example,) and relax in the bath for 20 minutes. Depending on individual preference, you can also place 1 spoonful of bee honey and herbs such as rosemary, thyme and/or sage in a sachet and hang it in the tub. Or you could pour in a small cup of cream or a glass of milk. This treatment is particularly recommended for people with dry skin. If you suffer from dry skin on you back, brush your back dry first. The bath makes the scales of skin peel off and cleanses clogged pores more easily.

FOOT SOAK: If you are tired and overburdened, soaking your feet can be refreshing. Fill the tub up to your ankles with cold water and add ½ a cup of vinegar. For safety, there should be a non-slip mat on the tub bottom. Then soak your feet in the tub without moving or walk up and down in the water. You should continue soaking your feet for 5 to 10 minutes and, if you want, give them a warm or a cold shower.

Vinegar makes your hair shine

Anything good for the skin is good for the hair. Vinegar can also be used for hair care. Again, there are various possibilities for use.

Shampoo: your hair will get a special shine if shampoo is diluted with apple vinegar. Six teaspoons of vinegar are recommended for 2 cups of shampoo. Add vinegar to the shampoo slowly. Shampoo and vinegar tend to separate so you should shake the shampoo bottle well before using.

Rinsing: rinsing with vinegar makes dull hair shine. Put 3 tablespoons of vinegar into 2 cups of water. After washing and rinsing the hair, apply this mixture. Long hair can be combed more easily if you add some vinegar to the water when rinsing.

Vinegar ingredients

SIMILAR INGREDIENTS

All varieties of vinegar contain acetic acid dissolved in water. In common types of vinegar, the content of acetic acid ranges from 5% to 6%. In addition to the previously mentioned processes of vinegar production, acetic acid can also be produced chemically. For this purpose acetylene, a gas used in oil chemistry, is transformed to acetic aldehyde and then to acetic acid. This synthetic vinegar is highly concentrated and its acidic content ranges from 60% to 80%. The strong dilutions used in chemistry classes are also used industrially. These synthetic varieties of vinegar do not contain flavoring ingredients. Synthetic varieties of vinegar consist only of acetic acid and water. All other types of vinegar made by natural fermentation contain other ingredients.

THE SOURCE DETERMINES THE INGREDIENTS

Vinegar can be produced biologically from many basic ingredients: grape mash, grape juice, wine, apples and other types of fruit, brandy, beer, sherry or even whey or rice. The basic ingredients depend on the production process and storage. Generally, only a couple of rules need be remembered, but, as always, there are exeptions. THE MORE NATURAL the vinegar production, the richer the vinegar will be, no matter how small the quantity.

PASTEURIZED VINEGAR does not contain active acetic acid bacteria because they die during pasteurization.

There is generally less pulp in purified vinegars than in naturally thick vinegars. The pulp consists mainly of pectin and vegetable matter. Depending on the type of vinegar, a small number of vitamins, minerals and trace elements may be present, but the actual amount of any nutrient is usually exaggerated. Daily consumption of vinegar cannot provide enough nutrition to meet the minimum requirements.

VINEGARS stored in wooden barrels for a long time contain tannin and tannic acid and may protect against heart disease and cancer. However, such statements are old wives' tales and should not be taken too seriously.

Vinegar in the household

VINEGAR AS A CLEANING LIQUID: Put a dose of vinegar in your dishwashing water and you will have clean and shiny dishes while using less dish detergent. The dishwasher detergent can also be replaced with vinegar.

Very persistent dirt on pots and pans can be easily removed using vinegar. Soak the pots in vinegar for half an hour before washing to loosen the fat and the remaining dried food. Vinegar is also useful for the decalcification of small kitchen appliances. Limescale stains on water kettles and teapots are stubborn. You can remove the stains using a mixture consisting of 2 parts vinegar to 1 part water with some salt. Boil the mixture briefly and soak for one night to loosen the deposits. You should decalcify your kettles and teapots regularly to extend the life of the appliances and save energy.

Thermos bottles, teapots and coffee pots that have tough brown spots and unpleasant smells can be cleaned by washing in warm, lightly salted vinegar solution and then cleaning with a brush. Afterwards, rinse with boiling water.

OVEN AND REFRIGERATOR: Both appliances should be cleaned regularly with vinegar solution. Tough, burned-on stains in the oven can be removed easily with a cloth saturated with vinegar. Cleaning kitchen appliances with vinegar will disinfect them and remove unpleasant smells.

STAINS ON STAINLESS STEEL AND ALUMINUM POTS: If you put aluminum pots or cutlery into a boiling vinegar and water solution (1 tablespoon vinegar in each cup of water), any stains will disappear. Cleaning with a vinegar-saturated cloth makes cutlery and kitchen appliances shine again.

DULL GLASSES: Wash with water containing vinegar and your glasses will look new again. Approximately half a cup of vinegar for 4 liters of water is enough.

BREAD BIN: If you wash the bread bin once a week with vinegar solution, the bread stays fresh longer and does not lose its natural aroma. Vinegar absorbs bad smells and stops the growth of mold.

ONION AND GARLIC ODOR ON HANDS: You can avoid these president smells on your hands if you rub your hands with vinegar before and after peeling, cutting or chopping.

MINERAL STAINS IN THE TUB: Mineral stains in the tub and sink can be removed easily with vinegar. Soak a cloth in vinegar and wipe off the dirty spots. Blocked faucet heads and showerheads should be soaked in vinegar for a couple of hours and then brushed vigorously. Dirty toothbrush holders and shower doors can be easily cleaned as well.

CALCIUM IN THE WASHING MACHINE: Did you know that calcium shortens the lifetime of your washing machine? Add a cup of vinegar to each wash load to remove residual soap better. In any case, vinegar is an efficient addition to detergent that can replace fabric softener and can make the laundry fresh and soft. Wool clothes will be less stiff if they are rinsed in vinegar solution.

CLEANING WINDOWS: Every homeowner likes clean windows. Windowpanes and other glass items will be freed of smudges and streaks if they are cleaned with vinegar. For this purpose, use a mixture of equal amounts of vinegar and lukewarm water.

TOBACCO ODOR REMOVAL: Imagine that you have a party and you are a non-smoker. When the party is over, put a small open jar of vinegar in the room. Vinegar will absorb the tobacco odors. Try it after your next party.

MOTH-RIDDEN CURTAINS AND WALL HANGINGS: If you brush the carpets with a concentrated vinegar solution, it will not only clear away the moths, but will also restore the brightness of the fabric colors. Be careful not to soak the carpet too much.

CUT FLOWERS: Cut flowers will remain fresh longer if you add 2 tablespoons of vinegar and 2 tablespoons of sugar to the vase water. Put the flowers in the vase only after the water has reached room temperature and you can enjoy them for longer.

Flies and other insects: A regular application of equal amounts makes flies, moths, and other insects stay away.

Residual salt on shoes: You can remove salt lines on your boots and shoes with a small sponge soaked in a mix of equal amounts of vinegar and water.

How to make vinegar

As you read in the previous chapters, vinegar production is quite simple. Our grandmothers and great-grandmothers made vinegar on their own. You can make it as well, althogh you will have to be patient.

HOME PRODUCTION OF VINEGAR

You will need to buy white or red wine, preferably organic wine to ensure that the sulfur content is low. If possible, buy it directly from the vineyard or winery. Ask whether the wine is mildly sulfuric or not sulfuric at all, and if it is suitable for making vinegar.

You need a bulbous jar made of ceramic or glass. Wash it thoroughly and pour in 4 cups of wine. The jar should be covered with gauze or a permeable cotton cloth so that no flies or dust particles can get inside.

It is important to place the jar in a warm, dimly lit area. Acetic acid bacteria prefer temperatures of about 75° to 82° F. If the temperature drops too rapidly, the bacteria become inactive and no acid is formed. Remember that the bacteria die at extremely high temperatures and that the acetic process is ruined by other, undesired bacteria.

After a couple of days, a pectin layer is formed. This is a gelatin-like, sticky mush where the acetic acid bacteria live. It must not get wet or pressed down. If it disappears, the acetic acid bacteria can no longer take in the oxygen to produce acetic acid and die.

This amount of vinegar will be ready after 5 or 6 weeks. If there is more, between 12 to 16 cups, the process takes from 8 to 12 weeks.

The vinegar must be poured through a porous cloth or a coffee filter and put into clean, dry bottles.

Homemade vinegar is not pasteurized and therefore it is not completely free of acetic acid bacteria after filtering. If you do not want it to become more sour, put it into the refrigerator or another cool place to be sure that the bacteria do not become active.

Homemade apple vinegar

The production of apple vinegar is a bit more complicated because the oxidization must be preceded by alcohol fermentation.

Take between 3 and 6 lbs of apples; wash and dry them thoroughly. Cut them into slices and put them through a juicer.

Pour the apple juice into a ceramic jug or a glass demijohn. Add yeast (wine yeast) and seal the jar with a balloon or a plastic bag with a conservation ring. Everything must be sealed airtight. Carbon dioxide, formed during the alcohol fermentation, needs space. That is why the balloon or the bag swells. Alcohol fermentation takes place only if oxygen is kept out for 2 to 6 weeks, and the temperature should be between 77° to 82°F. The result is an alcoholic a cider or an apple wine.

The apple wine must now be treated as for the production of wine vinegar. You can leave the apple wine in the original jar, but plenty of air must now circulate around the liquid. You need a wide jar, such as a demijohn, which can be two-thirds full in the bulbous part of the bottle.

MAKING FLAVORED VINEGAR

Flavored vinegar is a term for varieties of vinegar containing herbs, spices or fruits. There is not much that can go wrong during the flavoring process because the process is fast and simple, and needs less space and equipment than the original vinegar process.

Particularly suitable base vinegars are distilled vinegar and wine vinegar. Naturally, you can also dilute acetic substances with water and mix them in a ratio of 1:1.

The flavoring process is quite simple and in principle the same for every type of vinegar. Seasonings such as spices, fruits, or herbs are washed thoroughly and diced in order to help the flavors escape into the vinegar more effctively. Then they are placed in a clean bottle or a screw top jar. The jar is filled with vinegar and the mixture is left at room temperature for at least a couple of days, and sometimes up to 4 weeks. Vinegar dissolves flavors and colors from the added ingredients. Taste the vinegar occasionally and decide when it has achieved the right flavor. Sometimes it is necessary to filter the vinegar to remove undissolved ingredients such as bits of fruit or onions. Other seasoned or herb vinegars look nice with the undissolved ingredients floating in the bottle. As long as the ingredients are submerged in the vinegar, they can simply be left in the bottle, but if they are exposed, baceria or mold could start to grow on them, spoiling the vinegar's flavor.

DELICIOUS FLAVORED VINEGARS

APPLE AND LEMON BLAM VINEGAR: fruit vinegar; 2 small, sweet apples, peeled and diced; 4 sprigs lemon balm, chopped finely

PEAR AND CINNAMON VINEGAR: red wine vinegar; 1 Williams pear, peeled and diced; 2 cinnamon sticks; 2 pieces star anise; 3 peppercorns.
Filter when the vinegar tastes strong enough for you.

ORANGE GINGER VINEGAR: white wine vinegar; 1 orange, freshly squeezed; 1 in piece of ginger, peeled and cut finely; 4 tablespoons honey.
Filter when the vinegar tastes strong enough for you.

LOVE VINEGAR: white wine vinegar; 1 handful rose flowers from your own garden; 2 shoots lavender flowers, not sprayed.
Filter when the vinegar tastes strong enough for you.

CRANBERRY VINEGAR: distilled vinegar; 3½ oz chopped cranberries; 3 tablespoons maple syrup.
Filter when the vinegar tastes strong enough for you.

"FINE HERB" VINEGAR: white wine vinegar; 3 shoots tarragon; half a bunch chives; 8 shoots parsley.
Filter when the vinegar tastes strong enough for you.

GARLIC VINEGAR: distilled vinegar; 10 garlic cloves, peeled and quartered;
1 teaspoon black peppercorns, ground in a mortar;
1 bay leaf, torn at the edges to release the oils.
Filter when the vinegar tastes strong enough for you.

CHILI VINEGAR: distilled vinegar; 2 red chili peppers, cut lengthwise; 3 garlic cloves, peeled and quartered; 1 teaspoon cumin, ground in a mortar.
Filter when the vinegar tastes strong enough for you.

The recommended amount is always for a wine bottle.

Aceto Balsamico

GENERAL CHARACTERISTICS: Aceto Balsamico is produced from boiled grape juice. But Aceto Balsamico is not a trademark and therefore cannot be precisely described. There are different types of balsamic vinegar, with various qualities. Aceto Balsamico is divided into four groups in this lexicon to eliminate some of the confusion concerning this product. However, the following classification has not been universally adopted:

- Aceto Balsamico tradizionale di Modena
- Aceto Balsamico tradizionale di Reggio Emilia
- Aceto Balsamico di Modena
- Aceto Balsamico

ACETO BALSAMICO TRADIZIONALE DI MODENA

GENERAL CHARACTERISTICS: The basic ingredient is a sugary white grape called Trebbiano, which does very well in the climate around Modena. The Trebbiano grapes should be picked as late as possible in the season, and must be picked by hand. Before pressing, the stems are removed and then the grapes are squeezed very gently so that the tannin content (from the skins and seed) is not too high.

PRESERVATION OF THE MUST: Before preserving, the sugar content in the juice is measured to ensure that it will make good vinegar. The juice is parboiled in an open kettle, and every vinegar-maker has his own method. It is important to keep the temperature below a maximum of 194°F so that the must does not caramelize, which would give it a burnt flavor. This process lasts many hours and requires patience and a lot of experience. When the must has cooled, and after the sediments have settled at the bottom, it is stored for the winter.

AGING OF BALSAMIC VINEGAR: To make vinegar from the thickened grape juice, you must first produce alcohol from the sugar, and then acetic acid from the alcohol. First, the juice is poured into wooden barrels. Traditionally, the first barrels have a volume of 53 gallons. In the course of aging, there are several stages before Aceto Balsamico tradizionale di Modena is formed. It must sit for at least 12 years in barrels that are progressively smaller in size and made of various types of wood. The volume of the last barrel must not be more than 5 gallons. Each vinegar-maker keeps the exact details of his aging process a closely-guarded secret.

GUARANTEE OF THE HIGHEST QUALITY: If a vinegar-maker says that his Aceto Balsamico is of good quality, and is determined to sell it as such, he must have it tasted by five independent members of a consortium. The consortium tests it for appearance, aroma and flavor to decide whether the product can be sold as Aceto Balsamico tradizionale di Modena. After the product has been approved, the vinegar is poured into half-cup, square-bottomed Giugiaro bottles. These bottles are always sealed with a pink test seal marked with a registration number. The vinegar-makers are then given their pure Aceto Balsamico back so they can label and mark it themselves.

DIFFERENT VARIETIES: The youngest vinegar of this type is 12 years old, but there are also 24-year-old and 48-year-old varieties available. The 100-year-old Aceto Balsamico tradizionale di Modena is an extreme example. The type of wooden barrel used will affect the vinedar's fla-

vor. Traditionally, oak, chestnut, robinia, ash, cherry, mulberry and juniper wood were used. Different types of wood are used in different combinations to alter the qualities of the vinegar. Chestnut wood is responsible for coloration and proper acid formation, while cherry wood makes it sweet and juniper adds a spicy flavor.

Aceto Balsamico tradizionale di Reggio Emilia

General characteristics: This variety of Aceto differs from Aceto Balsamico tradizionale di Modena in its origin. It is not produced in Modena, but in nearby Reggio Emilia. It is made from a higher number of grape varieties. In addition to Trebbiano, Occhio di gatto, Spergola, Berzemino and Lambrusco are used.

Preservation of must/storage: The differences are minimal. The vinegars are traditionally stored in barrels that give off a strong flavor. Therefore, this variety of Aceto is a little bit sharper and stronger. Its quality is also checked in the laboratory of the consortium of Aceto Balsamico tradizionale di Reggio Emilia producers. It is sold in thin, bulbous bottles marked with a seal and registration number.

ACETO BALSAMICO DI MODENA

In addition to pure Aceto Balsamico tradizionale di Modena, vinegars of all qualities are sold in Modena under the name "*Aceto Balsamico di Modena.*" You must ask your own palate if the vinegar is high in quality, as vinegar sold under this name is not subject to any special quality controls. There are many low-priced products that certainly have nothing in common with the traditionally-made Aceto Balsamico. How could a vinegar-maker produce high quality vinegar with traditional methods and still offer it at low prices? Very cheap vinegars are synthetic products probably made with thickened grape juice using the acetate method. The vinegars made this way are inexpensive, but they have nothing in common with traditional vinegar production in Modena. In Italy, rumor has it that much of the an Aceto for sale consists of an acetic acid solution, sugar pigment and artificial flavors because Italian law concerning food has not been enforced.

ACETO BALSAMICO

This variety of vinegar can be produced all over the world, as it is not a registered brand name. In the vinegar producing industry, an unspoken agreement has been made stating that the basic ingredient in all balsamic vinegar is preserved grape juice, and it depends on the pro-

ducer as to how it is processed afterwards. There are certainly vinegar producers outside Modena and Reggio
Emilia who make balsamic vinegar based on the classical method or who use the Schuezenbach method, storing the vinegar with other types of grapes. In any case,
low price industrial vinegar sold under the brand name
Aceto Balsamico has undoubtedly been made using the
acetate method and will not have been properly aged in
the barrel.

COMPOSITION: It is not possible to give exact information as Aceto Balsamico is analyzed for flavor, not chemical content. Both varieties of Aceto Balsamico tradizionale must contain highly-concentrated acid and countless wood and grape flavors and are therefore used sparingly. The cheaper the vinegar, the lower the concentration of its flavoring ingredients.

HISTORICALLY: People in Modena say that the original wine makers, who pressed grapes with their bare feet, supported themselves with sticks so as not to put all their weight on the grapes, or they let their children do the work because they weighed much less. It is incorrect to assume that Aceto was made in cellars. Vinegar needs a lot of air and it was traditionally stored in attics. Some vinegars are still stored under the roof.

SIDE NOTE: In 1994, about 10,000 bottles of Aceto Balsamico tradizionale were filled, i.e. about 264 gallons. In 1999, it was 1,374 gallons. In Italy, over 5,283 gallons of vinegar are produced each year.

COOKINGS TIPS

You should drizzle balsamic vinegar drop-by-drop on the food to complete the flavor.
The rule is: the cheaper the balsamic vinegar, the more you need to use. You can also use it to marinate meat, especially game.

IN COOKING

TASTE:

In terms of flavor, Aceto Balsamico tradizionale cannot be compared with common vinegar. It is spicier, sweeter, slightly sharp and somewhat oily. Very good types of ordinary Aceto Balsamico come close to the registered ones. The taste of Aceto Balsamicos is reminiscent of sweet red wine vinegar.

USE:

There is almost no dish that Aceto Balsamico will not complement. It is an indispensable part of northern Italian cuisine. It goes well with light salads, creamy risottos, pungently flavored venison dishes and thinly sliced roast beef. You will be also surprised by walnut ice-cream or panna cotta flavored with a few drops of delicious vinegar.

PURCHASE/STORAGE:

Aceto Balsamico tradizionale di Modena carries an exorbitant price. A half-cup bottle can cost more than $120. You can only buy it in delicacy shops or in good specialty stores selling oil and vinegar. The more common Aceto Balsamico is available in every supermarket at less than $2.50 for a full wine bottle. Both types should be stored in a dark area.

Warm Salmon carpaccio with chanterelles

Tip:
If you are not a fish fan, you can make it with roast beef and green pepper instead.

INGREDIENTS: 2 lbs salmon filet, center cut • 1 tablespoon olive oil • salt • pepper • 2 lbs chanterelles • half a bunch chives • 1 head Frisée lettuce • 2 oz pancetta or streaky bacon, cut in cubes • 2 tablespoons butter • about 2 tablespoons Aceto Balsamico

PREPARATION: Preheat the oven. Oil four plates and season with salt and pepper. Cut the salmon into thin slices and put them in a circle on the plates. Clean the chanterelles, rinse and drain. Cut the chives, wash and prepare the lettuce and squeeze it dry. Fry the bacon in a pan, remove it and keep warm. Add the butter to the pan. Add chanterelles, sauté, salt and sprinkle with chives. Put the plates of salmon in the oven for 10–15 seconds. Add the bacon and the lettuce to the salmon. Sprinkle with Aceto Balsamico.

Balsamic mushrooms

INGREDIENTS: ½ lb mixed lettuce (preferably oak leaf, field lettuce, radicchio, or chicory) • 4 small tomatoes • 1 lb small, white mushrooms • 4–5 tablespoons butter for sautéing • 4 tablespoons Aceto Balsamico • 2 tablespoons honey • salt • 2 large potatoes • oil for deep-frying

PREPARATION: Wash, drain and prepare the lettuce. Wash and quarter the tomatoes. Place on four plates. Clean the mushrooms, halve and sauté in butter. Salt, dash with Aceto Balsamico and sweeten with honey. Continue to cook until the mashrooms are lightly browned. Wash and peel the potatoes and cut into thin strips. Heat the oil to 356°F and deep-fry the potatoes until gold-brown. Remove, dry and salt. Arange the mushrooms on the lettuce and garnish with the fried potato strips.

Tip
You can use any type of wild mushroom, that can be cut into strips, or small chanterelles.

Wine vinegar

BASIC INGREDIENTS: Wine vinegar is made from wine, grape juice or grape mash.

ORIGIN OF THE BASIC INGREDIENTS: Wine is as old as vinegar and nobody knows its precise history. One thing that we know for sure is that growing wine grapes was popular by the year 3500 BC in Egypt, Babylon and India.

CHARACTERISTICS OF THE BASIC INGREDIENTS: As you know, wine is made from grapes. Varieties of grape, such as Riesling, Gray Burgundy and Silvaner, are used to made white wines. Blue Burgundy, Dornfelder and Portuguese are ideal for red wines. To make red wine, the pressed grapes are kept with the juice longer so that the pigment can be released more effectively and the must will be colored. Regardless of whether it is red or white must, part of the grape sugar must be fermented by yeast to alcohol in a tank, without oxygen. The grape must is processed to produce raw wine. In order to develop its full flavor, it must mature and be stored for a certain amount of time before it bottled. Depending on the variety, wine is processed to vinegar by adding acetic acid bacteria in various production methods (see the chapter „Production of Vinegar"). Vinegar makers usually buy prepared wine. Wine vinegar can also be made directly from grape juice or

mash using the same method by which alcohol is fermented.

HISTORICALLY: Wine vinegar was often a secondary product. It was invented accidentally while producing wine because acetic acid bacteria are present everywhere in the air. If the barrels are not hermetically sealed, alcohol is quickly oxidized to acetic acid. This process can be prevented by sulfurization. Acetic acid bacteria do not multiply in strongly sulfuric wine. For this reason, vinegar producers must desulfurize wine with hydrogen peroxide. In the past, wine vinegar was made in all households where grapes were grown. At the end of the 14th century, the first vinegar guild was founded near the town of Orleans.

DIFFERENT VARIETIES: Basically, wine vinegar can be divided into red and white varieties. A growing trend is vinegars made of only one type of grape.

COMPOSITION: Vinegar contains residual sugar, flavored substances and the essential mineral of wine production, potassium. Red wine vinegar, unlike white wine vinegar, is rich in tannin.

USE IN HERBAL MEDICINE: Wine vinegar is thought to stimulate digestion when consuming dishes high in calories. Vinegar packs were used in medieval herbal medicine to ease inflammation, swelling and bruises. The healing effect has now been scientifically confirmed because the evaporation of the vinegar has a cooling effect, and vinegar also disinfects the skin.

VINEGAR PACK

Soak a flexible cloth in a mixture made with wine vinegar and water in a 1:1 ratio. Wring the cloth out slightly and put it on the injured area. You should not put this type of pack on open wounds: although vinegar disinfects, it burns and there are more effective ways to treat wounds.

IN COOKING

TASTE:
Wine vinegars have a mildly sour taste. Red wine vinegar is often stronger in flavor than white wine vinegar. Depending on the quality and production processes, you can taste, to a greater or lesser extent, the basic ingredient: wine.

USE:
Pickled vegetables are often put into white wine vinegar. White wine vinegar goes well with salads whose ingredients have their own strong flavor. You can also flavor fish with white wine vinegar instead of lemon juice.

PURCHASE/STORAGE:
You will find cheap wine vinegars in every supermarket. Special wine vinegars made with only one type of grape and aged in a barrel for very long periods are available in well-stocked wine stores and in stores specializing in oil and vinegar. If wine vinegar is stored well-sealed in a dark area, its shelf life is virtually unlimited.

COOKING TIPS:
White wine vinegar is particularly suitable for flavoring with herbs. If you preserve strawberries, you can make the flavor of the jam, stronger by adding one teaspoon of red wine vinegar for every 2 lbs of fruit.

Arugula-avocado-salad

Tip
This salad also goes well with vinaigrette made with blue cheese, white wine vinegar, and walnut oil.

INGREDIENTS: 3 ½ oz arugula • 1 ripe avocado • 5 cherry tomatoes • 10 pickled pumpkin pieces • 3 spicy pickles • 1 teaspoon capers • 1 teaspoon mustard • 1 teaspoon white wine vinegar • 2 tablespoons olive oil • salt and a little sugar

PREPARATION: wash the arugula, drain dry and tear into bite-sized pieces. Peel the avocado, remove the stone and cut the flesh into strips. Put the arugula and the avocado on plates. Cut the cherry tomatoes into quarters, dice the pumpkin and spicy pickles. Chop the capers unevenly. Mix the capers carefully with the mustard, white wine vinegar and olive oil. Add salt and sugar to taste. Pour the dressing over the salad.

Turkey, strawberry, arugula kebobs

INGREDIENTS: 1 lb turkey breast • 1 chili pepper • 4 tablespoons soy sauce • 1 tablespoon honey• 4 tablespoons red wine vinegar • 1 pinch salt• 2 tablespoons sunflower oil • 1 lb strawberries • 1 bunch arugula • 12 kebob skewers

Tip
Instead of strawberries, use other types of fruit such as peaches.

PREPARATION: Rinse the meat, dry and dice. Wash the chili, halve, remove the seeds and mince. Mix the soy sauce with the honey, red wine vinegar and minced chili. Add salt to the meat and marinate for 1 hour. Heat the oil and cook the meat in it. Wash the strawberries and arugula and skewer alternately with the pieces of meat on the skewers.

Vineyard vinegar

A person who shops at a winery expects to find quality wine. However, did you know that many wineries also sell vinegar? There is a stubborn conception that wine vinegar is made with low-quality wine. It is certainly true that industrially made wine vinegar, which costs around $1.50 in a supermarket, cannot be made with expensive wine. However, vineyard vinegars are produced from high quality wines and in small quantities. They are fermented for a long time using the surface method and then stored in old wine barrels to develop an especially full flavor.

WHAT DOES A WINERY DO WITH THE WINE?

Wine vinegar is made with wine grapes grown in the producer's own vineyard. It isusually sold directly by the winery. However, the wine producer may not wish to make vinegar on his own or at his own vineyard because there must be a strict separation between wine cellars and the place where vinegar is made. Acetic acid bacteria are not desired at vineyards because one mistake can quickly turn the wine to vinegar.

Therefore, a lot of wineries have their original wines processed to vinegar elswhere, for a fee. A real master of the production of wine vinegars is Robert Bauer, who has specialized in high quality wine vinegars for more than 20 years in his firm Acetoria. He produces pure vinegars under his brand name or at the request of wineries, wine-producing companies or large state wine producers. Only pure varieties of wine are used to make vinegar. You will not only find "white wine" or "red wine" vinegar on the label, but a detailed description of the basic ingredients as well. Very tasty vinegars are made from quality wines, offering a wide range of flavors.

FLAVOR EXPERIENCE IN THE BROAD SENSE OF THE WORD

Wine vinegars are a must in fine cuisine, useful for dressing salads and preserving. Flavorful gravies, as well as fish and vegetables, are enhanced by pure vineyard vinegars. Some of these vinegars are also drunk, before or after the meal as an aperitif or a digestive, or with chocolate.

Malt vinegar

BASIC INGREDIENTS: Malt vinegar is made with beer or beer mash.

ORIGIN OF THE BASIC INGREDIENTS: Beer is made with malt (sprouted barley) and yeast. Barley is a cereal which has been grown in central Europe since the early Stone Age. Beer was brewed from barley in ancient Egypt.

CHARACTERISTICS OF THE BASIC INGREDIENTS: Barley is an annual grass. It differs from other types of grains in its long beards (hair on the seeds). After the harvest, barley is chopped, dried and malted by adding water. Barley mash is produced. The starch in the grains is dissolved and it has a pleasant, sweet smell. Yeast is added to the mash and left to ferment in large tanks where there is no oxygen. Alcohol forms. The more alcohol beer contains, the faster it can ferment to vinegar because it must reach 5% acetic acid, depending on the alcohol content of the original beer.

Making malt vinegar demands a lot of practice because beer contains a great deal of protein which must be removed before the bacteria are introduced. The carbonic acid must also be removed from the beer.

HISTORICALLY: In warmer parts of Europe, barley has used less and less in bread since the Middle Ages. However, it has been increasingly used in beer production as beer gradually replaced mead as the main drink in northern Europe. Malt vinegar was produced in every brewery because beer and malt both have limited durability and acetic acid bacteria causes vinegar to be formed easily in the open air. Vinegar pickling was, in addition to salting and smoking, one of the few preservation methods available at that time. The demand for vinegar was extremely high and meat and fish were pickled as well as vegetables.

DIFFERENT VARIETIES: As there are different types of beer, there are also various types of malt vinegar. German malt vinegars are made with a particular type of beer, such as Pilsner, Kölsch, or Bock. Other malt vinegars are made from the malt in the first stage of beer.

COMPOSITION: compared to other types of vinegar, malt vinegar contains more vitamin B2 and protein than beer. The protein content is below 0.018 ounce per half/cup.

In cooking

Taste:

Malt vinegar smells like beer. It is mildly sour and herbal. You can taste its beer flavor. Depending on the type of beer used, it can have a light or dark amber color. Malt vinegar is dark and a bit sweet, but pleasantly sour.

Use:

Malt vinegar is a classic in Pommersche kielbasa, sour pickled carp and other forgotten specialties of German cuisine such as hearty Bavarian fish dishes. In northern countries, fried fish is usually seasoned with malt vinegar as are French fried potatoes. Savory pies and pastries also taste good with malt vinegar

Purchase/Storage:

Beer vinegar is a rarity. It is only available in oil and vinegar stores. The shelf life of beer vinegar is virtually unlimited. The bottle should be stored in the dark and sealed so that its color and flavor do not alter. Malt vinegar can be found in most Supermarkets.

Cooking tip:

If you invite guests for an evening of Scottish or Scandinavian cooking, you should not forget to offer malt vinegar for a truly authentic touch.

Lentil soup with tomatoes and bacon

INGREDIENTS: half a cup dry brown lentils • 1 bottle Altbeer • 1 medium-sized onion • 3 oz smoked streaky bacon • 1 tablespoon oil • 2 pints bouillon (instant) • 1 bay-leaf • 1 bunch soup greens (1 lb) • 1 lb potatoes • 1 can or 2 cups tomatoes • salt • ground pepper • 1 tablespoon German beer vinegar

PREPARATION: Let the lentils soak in the Altbeer for 3–4 days. Peel and dice the onion. Slice the bacon into medium-sized cubes. Heat the oil in a pot. Fry the bacon and onion. Add the lentils with their soaking liquid, the bouillon and the bay-leaf. Let boil for 25–30 minutes. Wash, prepare and dice the soup greens. Wash, peel and dice the potatoes. Add the vegetables and potatoes 10 minutes before finishing the soup. Drain and dice tomatoes, then add to the soup and cook for 1 minute. Season with salt, pepper and vinegar. Remove the bay-leaf and pour the soup into bowls. Altbeer goes well with the dish.

Ground pork and onion loaf

INGREDIENTS: 1 day-old bread roll • 1 lb mixed ground meat • 1 lb raw pork • 2 bread eggs (medium-sized) • salt • ground pepper • 4 medium-sized tomatoes • 1 medium-sized onion (approximately 1 lb) • herbs for garnishing • 4 tablespoons malt vinegar • fat for the baking sheet

PREPARATION: Soak the bread roll in cold water for 10 minutes. Squeeze thoroughly and mix with the ground meat, pork and eggs to make smooth mixture. Season with salt and pepper. Place the ground mixture on an oiled baking sheet and form into a flat rectangle (approximately 12 x 8 in). Wash and prepare the tomatoes and onion and cut them into thin slices. Garnish the ground mixture with the tomatoes and the onion, salt and pepper. Bake the loaf for 40–45 minutes in a preheated oven at 392°F. Then cut it into pieces and serve on a plate, garnished with herbs and sprinkled with malt vinegar. Beer goes well with this dish.

Distilled vinegar

BASIC INGREDIENTS: This variety of vinegar, also know sa white vinegar is made with alcohol

ORIGIN OF THE BASIC INGREDIENTS: Alcohol is distilled from sugar beet, sugar cane, berries, fruits, grains or potatoes. Rye brandy, vodka, whiskey and rum can be used for producing alcohol vinegar.

CHARACTERISTICS OF THE BASIC INGREDIENTS: The distillation of alcohol is a multi-stage process. First, the basic ingredients must be processed to condense the sugar. That means that the fruit must be broken down, the molasses must be extracted from sugarbeets or the grains must be malted. To get alcohol from the basic ingredients, it is necessary to add yeast, which transforms sugar into alcohol. To increase the alcohol content and improve the flavor of the alcohol, the mash is distilled. All of the ingredients are gently boiled while the alcohol and its flavor components are vaporized more quickly than water from the mash. The alcohol and evaporated flavor components are accumulated and cooled again, resulting in the formation of highly concentrated alcohol which is then diluted to reach an alcohol content of 32% to 40%. If vinegar is made using the surface or Schuezenbach method, the final distilled vinegar contains

from 5% to 14% acid. When producing white vinegar using the acetate method, the desired acidic content in alcohol vinegar is determined with careful monitoring thoughout the production process.

DIFFERENT VARIETIES: Distilled vinegar is a very commn and versatile vinegar. It is used in many prepared sauces, such as ketchup and grill sauces, as well as in mayonnaise and pickled foods. Vinegar that is made using the surface or Schuezenbach method is a real handmade vinegar, and unlike synthetic vinegar, its flavor nuances are perserved. A particular specialty is whiskey vinegar. Well-made whiskey vinegars have a peaty flavor. You might also enjoy the fruity flavor of vinegar made with fruit brandy.

COMPOSITION: As a rule, distilled vinegar contains 5% acid. Its acid content is marked on the bottle just as with other vinegars. Distilled vinegar contains no substances of interest other than flavoring ingredients. It may still contain 0-5% alcohol.

POTATO VINEGAR: In principle, potato vinegar is not made with potatoes, but with vodka. This type of vinegar originated among Russian peasants. Even now, people in rural Russia distil vodka themselves. Some of the vodka is watered down and processed into vinegar. Russian delicacies, such as gherkins, capers and beets, are pickled in it. The terms "distilled vinegar" or "vodka vinegar" would certainly be more appropriate, but it is known as potato vinegar.

IN COOKING

TASTE:
Distilled vinegar has a simple, classic vinegar taste. It may be sharper or smoother depending on its production method, base alcohol and producer.

USE:
For a long time, distilled vinegar has been regarded as a kitchen essential. One spoonful of this vinegar is a standard flavoring for lentil soup. However, certain more delicate dishes, such as homemade mayonnaise or cold sauces, are often flavored with a distilled vinegar as well.

PURCHASE/STORAGE:
Distilled vinegar is available in every good supermarket. To buy particularly pure distilled vinegars, you must go to a delicatessen or specialty store that sells oil and vinegar. You should store distilled vinegar hermetically sealed in a dark area.

COOKING TIPS
Distilled vinegar goes very well with dishes with strong flavors. Put one spoonful of distilled vinegar into boiling water for eggs and they will not crack so quickly. Distilled vinegar is the most common vinegar for pickled cucumbers and sour vegetables.

Pickled tomatoes

INGREDIENTS: 2 lbs fleshy tomatoes • 12 spring onions • 2 cloves garlic • 3 tablespoons basil oil • 1 tablespoon distilled vinegar • 1 or 2 teaspoons dried Italian herbs • 1 teaspoon raw sugar • salt • pepper

PREPARATION: Peel, quarter and core the tomatoes. Peel the onions, tear off the green parts and halve. Peel the garlic and slice thinly. Preheat the oven to 347°F. Fill a high-slided baking pan with 1 inch of water. Heat the oil in a large pot, briefly sweating the onions and garlic. Add the tomato pieces, vinegar, herbs, sugar, salt and pepper. Stir while heating. Heat the vegetables about 15 minutes, stirring occasionally. Season to taste. Pour into four oven safe glasses (holding about half a cup) and put on the baking sheet. Bake on the lowest rack of the oven. When the tomatoes start boiling, reduce the temperature of the oven to 302°F. After 30 minutes, take the jars out of the oven, seal and allow to cool.

Spiced pickles

INGREDIENTS: half a cup salt • 6 cups water • 3 – 4 lbs pickling cucumbers • 6 small onions • 5 cups distilled vinegar • 3 cups water • juice from 2 lemons • half a cup sugar • 2 ½ oz salt • some dill tops • 1 tablespoon white peppercorns • 2 bay leaves • 4 cloves

PREPARATION: Rinse and brush the pickling cucumbers carefully, put them into salted water and set in a cool place. Chop the onions roughly. Boil the vinegar, water, lemon juice, salt and sugar together. Drain the water, rinse and dry the cucumbers thoroughly. Put the cucumbers, pieces of onion, peppercorns, dill tops, cloves and bay-leaves into jars, fill the jars to the rim with the boiling vinegar solution and seal immediately. Let the spiced pickles stand for about 4 to 6 weeks in a cool, dark place.

Champagne vinegar

BASIC INGREDIENTS: Champagne vinegar is made from champagne.

ORIGIN OF THE BASIC INGREDIENTS: Champagne has been a registered trademark since the Versailles Treaty was signed in 1919. Champagne refers to sparkling wines from the Champagne region of France. The basic wine is produced from red grape wines, such as Pinot Noir or Pinot Meunier, as well as from white wine, such as Chardonnay. The basic wine is poured into bottles and the "Liqueur de triage" is added: a mixture is made from wine, sugar and special types of yeast. Champagne matures in the bottle after having been shaken and corked. The neck of the bottle is dipped in an ice cold bath and the yeast is frozen so that when you open the bottle, the yeast plug flies out. The legends about champagne say that it was invented by a Benedictine monk named Dom Pérignon in the Hautvillers by Epernay abbey. After the death of the wine-master Pérignon, the first sparkling wines appeared in the 18th century. Champagne appeared in a variety of flavors. The English wine producers had problems selling wine with the fine sharp flavor of Champagne to the country people, so they added sugar because they did not realize that alcohol fermentation would start again. The carbon dioxide could not evaporate and it remained in the bottle. But the whole world, including the English, started to like the beautiful, sparkling drink.

CHARACTERISTICS OF THE BASIC INGREDIENTS: Champagne vinegar is more stringently protected by law than champagne itself. That is why there are countless vinegars of champagne, but not all of them can be described as "champagne vinegar." To make vinegar from champagne, the carbonic acid must first be removed because acetic acid bacteria are very sensitive to champagne. Then the champagne is treated like normal wine vinegar, made using both the acetate and surface methods. A good reason to use the acetate method is that after long periods of storage in barrels, the finer flavors of the champagne are influenced by wood flavors. A person who likes the combination of the wood and the champagne flavors should choose more expensive vinegar. In addition to vinegar made with pure champagne, there are also vinegars which are made with one cuvée (mixture) of wine from three traditional types of champagne grapes. Even though champagne was a basic ingredient, this type of blended champagne vinegar is cheaper than pure champagne vinegar. Pure champagne vinegar is expensive because the vinegar producer must pay for the bottle of pure champagne.

Different varieties: The names "Champagne" and "Methode champenoise" were banned outside the region of Champagne by the European Union on 13 July 1992 in accordance with the judicial decision of the European Tribunal for Sparkling Wines. Consequently, champagne vinegar sold in the European Union must be 100% produced in Champagne.

Composition: The acidic content in champagne vinegar varies between 6 and 8% and its content is marked on the bottle, as with any other variety. Champagne vinegar is also subject to wine regulations. In addition to water and acid, it contains alcohol and is not bound by the maximum amount of 0.5% as other vinegars are.

In cooking

Taste:
Champagne vinegar tastes pleasant and is mildly sour. It includes the fresh crispness and sharpness of champagne.

Use:
Like sherry vinegar or Aceto Balsamico tradizionale, champagne vinegar is a delicacy. Champagne fans like to improve dishes such as mango sorbet, light fish salad or bouillon with a drop of pure champagne vinegar.

Purchase/Storage:
Champagne vinegar is available only in delicacy shops. Since a $25-$37 bottle of champagne is generally suspect, be careful with prices under $18.50 for one bottle of champagne vinegar. In any case, champagne vinegar should be stored in a dark area and properly sealed.

Cooking tip:
You should season hot dishes with champagne vinegar only after cooking. Vinegar should not be boiled, or its flavor will evaporate.

Romaine salad with mango and Mozzarella

Tip:

Mango is ripe when the fruit flesh separates easily. You can also sprinkle the mango and melon cubes with champagne vinegar and let sit for 1 hour.

INGREDIENTS: 3 heads Romaine lettuce • 3 spring onions • half a bunch of lemon balm • half a Gallia melon • 1 mango • 3½ oz thinly sliced Parma ham • ½ lb small Mozzarella balls • 3 tablespoons champagne vinegar • 4 tablespoons sunflower oil • salt • ground black pepper

PREPARATION: Wash and prepare the Romaine lettuce heads and set aside 12 lettuce leaves. Cut the hearts into ½ in strips. Wash and prepare the onions and cut them into thin rings. Add onion rings to the lettuce strips. Wash and dry the the lemon balm. Tear the leaves off the stems and mince. Remove the melon seeds with a spoon. Scoop out balls from the melon and mix with the lettuce strips. Peel the mango. Separate the flesh of the fruit from the pit and dice. Cut the ham into strips and add it to the Mozzarella balls, lemon balm and pieces of melon and mango with the lettuce. Scrape the remaining melon pulp out of the rind with a spoon and purée. Mix half a cup of melon purée with champagne vinegar. Add oil, salt and pepper to the dressing. Pour over the salad.

Lemon gelatin with mango

INGREDIENTS FOR 2 PEOPLE: juice and peel from 2 lemons
• half a cup sugarless grapefruit juice • 2 tablespoons
Buckthorn juice (optional) • 1 drop champagne vinegar
• half a pack powdered gelatin • 1 mango

PREPARATION: Put the lemon juice in a small kettle. Add
the grapefruit and Buckthorn juices and heat slowly.
Season with a drop of champagne vinegar.
Mix the gelatin powder with 3 spoonfuls of cold water and
let it sit for 10 minutes. Stir the gelatin into the hot (but not
boiling) liquid and allow it to melt. Take the pot off the
stove and let the liquid cool. Pour the gelatin into 2 glass
bowls and let it cool for 3 hours. Before serving, peel the

mango, separate the fruit
from the core and cut it into
small pieces. Garnish the
cool lemon gelatin with the
pieces of mango.

Vinegar bonbons

A ROMANCE BETWEEN SWEET AND SOUR

Vinegar pralines, chocolate and vinegar! What an unusual combination! Sour vinegar and sweet chocolate – would this not challenge anyone's palate? After tasting vinegar drops, one of the great wine connoisseurs of the 20th century, Hugh Johnson, was forced to admit that the combination is "truly superb." What makes chocolate comboned with sour vinegar such a special experience?

CHOCOLATE – THE FOOD OF THE GODS

Cocoa beans originated in Central America. Chocolate was revered as a divine gift by Native Americans and reserved for priests and tribal chiefs. Chocolate came to Europe with the discovery of America. But Europeans did not like cocoa prepared without sugar as the Aztecs did. The name of this treat is actually derived from the Aztec xocoatl, a word comprised of xococ ('sour', 'herbal', 'spicy') and atl ('water'). With the addition of honey or raw sugar, the success of sweetened cocoa products spread around the world. Over time, the Aztec xocoatl became chocolate.

The Lucullan connection between Europe and America

A great love of chocolate and vinegar inspired the master confectioner Eberhard Schell to combine the two in one delicacy. With the addition of vinegar, chocolate got its splendid, rather sour, spicy, and herbal original flavor back. Eberhard Schell invented five particularly fine vinegar drops. The "Riesling Schleckerle" is a white or milk chocolate praline with vinegar made with late vintage Riesling and a crispy wafer. Vinegar candies made with Müller-Thurgau and covered with pure, bittersweet chocolate are very refreshing. Balsamic truffles melt irresistibly on the tongue. Mature balsamic vinegar goes well with bitter chocolate. The "Lemberger Schleckerle" combines the joy of fine chocolate with marzipan flavor and a few drops of Lemberger vintage vinegar. Although all of the delicacies mentioned contain vinegar and chocolate, it is difficult to compare them because each chocolate has something special and offers a unique experience.

Sherry vinegar

Although no other country produces as much wine vinegar as Spain, sherry vinegar has a very special place among the other splendid Balsamicos. Sherry vinegar is fermented from the best sherry wine produced in the region around Jerez de la Frontera. Based on the Solera method, the sherry is placed in an oak barrel that already contains old sherry vinegar, complete with all its flavors and aging bacteria. It is then left to ferment for a second time.

After aging, only a portion is poured out and the barrel is topped up with new vinegar. 100-year-old sherry vinegar becomes milder and more flavorful in its barrel year after year. Aging has a remarkable effect on the color: the older it is, the darker it becomes.

BASIC INGREDIENTS: As the name indicates, sherry vinegar is made with sherry. Sherry is made from three white grape varieties: Palomino, Pedro Ximénes and Muscatel. The Solera method matures the must to sherry.

ORIGIN OF THE BASIC INGREDIENTS: In the year 1000 BC, the Phoenicians founded the town of Xera, today's Jerez, and made wine. The source of sherry might have developed in the 13th or 14th centuries. Wine was fortified with

alcohol to preserve it longer. Fortified wine has acquired its fans. The British people in particular have helped wine from Jerez become world famous. They are even responsible for giving the wine its present name. Since the name of the town, "Jerez" was a tongue twister for English people, the wine became known as "Sherry", and the word was even adopted by Spanish people living in Andalusia.

CHARACTERISTICS OF THE BASIC INGREDIENTS: The composition of Jerez wine is different from that produced elsewhere because of the oxidized fermentation that takes place. During the production process, the wine is in contact with oxygen. The sherry base is stored during its formation in designated sizes of barrels.

Because it is changed regularly, and the barrels are not completely filled, the wine is given plenty of contact with

oxygen. Sometimes the oxygen contact is too sudden and, as a result, the sherry smells like ordinary vinegar rather than the desired sherry vinegar. Sherry vinegar is a product which must be produced meticulously.

Sherry should contain at least 11% alcohol. Sherry vinegar is produced in small quantities through the acetate method, or more rarely, using the Orleans method. The taste of the sherry vinegar is affected by the type of sherry: Fino, Manzanilla or Oloroso. Then, the sherry vinegar is stored in the Solera system, which is comprised of at least three steps. The barrels that are used to hold the sherry are made primarily of American oak because the wood has large pores which allow air to enter the liquid. The barrels are only filled to five-sixths of their volume. In the system, older, primary vinegar is poured into younger vinegar.

Sherry vinegar from Jerez is checked by a *Cosejo Regulador*. There are minimum requirements that the vinegar must meet. The wine must come from vineyards in close proximity to Jerez, and the vinegar production must also take place in the same region. There are two aging categories: "Vinagre de Jerez," which has matured at least 6 months, and "Vinagre de Jerez Reserva," which has matured at least 24 months.

DIFFERENT VARIETIES: Sherry vinegar is not a registered trademark. You can find sherry vinegar that has been imported from Canada. This vinegar only has certain basic ingredients in common with the original sherry. It is hard to imagine, considering its low price, that it was really stored in wooden barrels. You will usually find the address of the producer and the age, such as 25 or even 50, on a bottle of authentic sherry vinegar. These vinegars were stored in barrels for that time, and they are as dark as Aceto Balsamico tradizionale. They are usually only put into 1 cup bottles. Producers of other quality types state which type of sherry has been added, such as "Vinagre de Manzanilla."

COMPOSITION: Sherry vinegar from Jerez usually contains at least 7% acid. The amount of acid is marked on the bottle. The remaining alcohol level may be a maximum of 3%. The amount of residual sugar and flavored substances from the sherry can differ greatly. By adding sweet sherry, the sugar content increases. The longer the vinegar is stored using the Solera-system, the more water and alcohol vaporizes and the more concentrated the other flavored substances become.

SIDE NOTE: In Andalusia, about 85,000 gallons of sherry vinegar are produced per year. The quantity is really amazing, and sherry vinegar is only a secondary product because 30 times more sherry is produced. Alongside brandy, it is the most important exported culinary commodity in the region.

Gazpacho

Tip
*A soup garnish
made with
diced, hard-
boiled eggs is
also typical of
Gazpacho.*

INGREDIENTS: 3 slices white bread • 1 lb ripe tomatoes • 1 lb cucumber • 1 red pepper • 2 cloves garlic • 2 tablespoons olive oil • 2 tablespoons sherry vinegar • 2 tablespoons tomato puree • 1 cup tomato juice • 1 cup ice water • 2 teaspoons sugar • salt • black pepper

PREPARATION: Remove the bread crust, cut into small pieces, sprinkle with water and let stand for 30 minutes. Peel, pit and dice the vegetables. Put aside about 4 tablespoons of the cucumber and pepper. Peel the garlic and chop finely. Put the bread, vegetables and garlic in a blender. Add oil, sherry vinegar and tomato puree and blend to an even consistency. Add the tomato juice and ice water to the desired consistency. Let the soup cool for at least 1 hour and then cover it with a lid. Season with sherry vinegar, sugar, salt and pepper. Serve in soup bowls and garnish with the remaining cucumber and red pepper.

IN COOKING

TASTE:

Sherry vinegar has a pleasantly light, sour taste and a delicately woody flavor.

USE:

Sherry vinegar is an inseparable part of fine French cuisine and it has been traditionally established in the cuisine of the Andalusia region. It is a common seasoning for Tapas, Tortilla and Gazpacho, but it also goes well with light fish sauces and salad dressings.

PURCHASE/STORAGE:

Due to its production volume, sherry vinegar is cheaper than the king of vinegars, Aceto Balsamico tradizionale di Modena. High quality sherry vinegars are put into 1 cup bottles and are available for less than $6. Their shelf life is unlimited if they are stored, well-sealed, in the dark.

COOKING TIPS:

Did you know that there is a vinegar sprinkler? Filled with sherry vinegar, it can be used for sprinkling foie gras. Sherry vinegar goes very well with cloves and cinnamon in a sauce for veal or pork as well.

Herbal and spiced vinegars

BASIC INGREDIENTS: Herbal and spiced vinegars are vinegars with added flavoring. The base is made with wine or distilled vinegar containing dissolved herbs, spices or other flavors.

CHARACTERISTICS OF THE BASIC INGREDIENTS: Usually distilled vinegars are used to produce a particular flavored vinegar. Herbs, spices, flowers or food with strong flavors are added to the vinegar. Industrially processed herb vinegars are stored in cold, dark areas so that the vinegar is not tinted with chlorophyll from the leaves. Then, the vinegar is filtered and separated from the seasonings.

DIFFERENT VARIETIES: The most popular type of herb vinegar is made with common herbs, followed by tarragon vinegar. Fruit flavored vinegars are generally made with raspberries or currants. But there are also unusual varieties such as date vinegar made with Aceto Balsamico and date juice, plum vinegar made with red wine vinegar, plum compote and a touch of cinnamon, and cherry vinegar made with distilled vinegar, cherry purée and honey. You will also find herb vinegars made with wild garlic or flavored varieties such as jasmine vinegar, or vinegars made with rose and violet petals.

IN COOKING

TASTE:
The flavored vinegars should have a mildly sour flavor as well as the added taste. It is easy to identify the flavor of these vinegars.

USE:
Vinegars with added flavors are primarily used for salads. Some high quality vinegars are suitable as drinking vinegars as well. They should be served as an aperitif or as a digestive before or after a meal.

PURCHASE/STORAGE:
Common vinegars containing added flavors are available in every well-stocked supermarket. Special and natural flavors are available in specialty shops or in stores that sell vinegar and oil.

COOKING TIPS:
You will enjoy drinking vinegars stored at room temperature.

Time for Sour Sensuality

The vinegar farm

In the small village of Venningen, Pfalz, Doktorenhof farm produces wine vinegar. Doktorenhof, run by Georg Heinrich Wiedemann and his wife Johanna, is not just a common vineyard, as may be supposed from its location and surroundings in the heart of Germany's wine-making region. It is a small vinegar factory. At first sight, it seems an oasis of peace and pleasure. It is a special place where time stands still and where vinegar is made using the surface method. The charming, old buildings were once used as a vineyard by Georg Heinrich Wiedemann's parents. A good nose will smell the wonderful acidity of vinegar immediately upon entering the house.

How does an old vineyard become a small vinegar factory?

Reading old books and documents made Georg Wiedemann think about making his own vinegar. The Weidmans became passionate about vinegar production and have produced vinegar at Doktorenhof for 15 years. They still grow wine grapes today. They use high quality wine, even those from dry wine vintages, in their vinegars.

DRINKING VINEGAR – THE SPECIAL ART OF SOUR INDULGENCE

The Wiedemanns have developed an extraordinary love for vinegars containing added flavors. Their vinegars are refined with flowers, spices, herbs and roots. Creativity knows no bounds here! Doktorenhof offers wine vinegar made with jasmine petals, Portuguese vinegar with chestnut honey and vinegar made from white Burgundy and orange blossoms. Even adding dandelion honey or scented flowers is nothing special. With so many unique ingredients, it is not surprising that people are tempted to drink vinegar made by the Wiedemanns like wine. In fact, pure drops of vinegar have been a delicacy for ages. Vinegars intended for drinking have been served as an aperitif or a digestive for decades. For this purpose, special glasses for vinegar tasting have been developed. They have broad bottoms that narrow towards the top to funnel the flavors.

UP TO THE DOKTORENHOF

After making an appointment in advance, groups of visitors can come to see the Doktorenhof vinegar cellar and take part in vinegar tasting, just like wine tasting at a winery. In a vinegar room, you will be presented with a wide range of products: pure vinegar in decorated, blown glasses, vinegar sprinklers, vinegar mustard, vinegar gelatin, vinegar candies, vinegar coffee and much more. Art lovers must have a look at the colorful vinegar-oil pictures.

Trout with meadow herbs

INGREDIENTS: 4 fresh trout ½ lb • 4 thick bunches of freshly picked herbs (nettle, sour dock, clover, dandelion, nasturtium, peppermint) • 1 bunch parsley • 1 bunch chervil • 1 cup white wine • 1 cup vegetable broth • 1 ½ cups black elder vinegar • salt

PREPARATION: Wash the herbs and place half in a large saucepan. Wash and drain the trout, dry lightly with a clean dishcloth. Then, salt on both sides. Put the fish in a pot with the herbs and cover it with the other half of the herbs. Pour wine, broth and vinegar over it. Cover the pot and seal with aluminum foil. Bring to a boil and simmer for 15 minutes. Serve on a warmed plate with fresh herbs and butter.

Wiedemann:
"These recipes come from the kitchen of Giacomo Casanova. We have a special Casanova vinegar that we introduced for culinary evenings with invited guests. We prepare similar programs regularly."

Chocolate lasagne
with cappuccino sauce

INGREDIENTS: ½ lb boiled and peeled chestnuts • 1½ cups sugar • 1 tablespoon coffee bean vinegar • 2½ cups cream • ½ cup heavy cream • 2 cups bitter chocolate sauce • 1 cup white chocolate sauce • 4 tablespoons mocha powder • 2 tablespoons mocha liqueur

PREPARATION: Purée the chestnuts, 3½ tablespoons of sugar, coffee bean vinegar, 3 tablespoons of cream and add the heavy cream, mixing until creamy. Let it sit. Melt the chocolate sauces in water, spread a thin layer on a baking sheet with oiled paper, let cool and cut out rings with a pastry cutter. To make the cappuccino sauce, bring the remaining cream, sugar, mocha powder and liqueur to boiling point and simmer for 10 minutes. Alternately layer slices of the chocolate and the chestnut mousse. Garnish with fresh raspberries and mint.

Wiedemann:
"Sweet and sour unite in the dish like man and woman at night."

Apple cider vinegar

PRIMARY INGREDIENT: apple cider vinegar is made from apples in the form of apple juice, cider or apple wine.

ORIGIN OF THE BASIC INGREDIENTS: Apples are a truly multicultural fruit. The apple is a hybrid of numerous species of Malus (a subclass of Rosaceae), including the European wild apple and the domesticated Chinese love apple. According to evidence uncovered in villages of the mound-builder period, apples were picked wild in these latitudes during the early Stone Age.

GENERAL CHARACTERISTICS: Apples are the most important fruit in mild climate zones. There are now over 20,000 varieties. It is important for the production of apple cider vinegar that apples with an optimal ripeness are picked. The sugar content should be as high as possible. The fruit is pressed and left to ferment into cider and then to apple cider vinegar. The quality of the primary ingredient is critical for the quality of apple cider vinegar. The price of the vinegar depends on the quality. Certainly, the most expensive type of apple cider vinegar is one produced from a single type of apple. The next quality level is apple cider vinegar made of freshly pressed apple juice consisting of many types of apples. There are other apple cider vinegars made of preserved apple juice or ap-

ple juice concentrate. Sometimes the apple juice is not sweet enough and sugar or a sugar solution is added or mixed with water and sugar. In either case, it must ferment to alcohol before the acetic acid oxidization starts.

HISTORICALLY: The Phoenicians traditionally made apple cider vinegar wherever a lot of apple trees were planted. The apples or cider were used for making vinegar in households.

DIFFERENT TYPES: In addition to the above mentioned criteria, apple cider vinegar can be divided into vinegar containing natural pulp and filtered vinegar. The natural pulp is preferable to clear vinegar because the pulp is not a sign of bad quality, as many people believe.

Although it is not common, "apple cider vinegar" can be a blend of apple cider vinegar and wine vinegar or distilled vinegar. Any foodstuff consisting of more than one ingredient has to have a list of ingredients. You can judge vinegar according its list of ingredients. If the label on the bottle reads "apple cider vinegar," and there is no list of ingredients, it is pure apple cider vinegar made with cider.

COMPOSITION: Apple cider vinegar contains 5% acid, which is noted on each bottle of vinegar. The content of residual alcohol can be 0.5%, as with most other types of vinegar. Cider vinegar also contains residual sugar, flavoring, potassium and vitamin C from the cider. Pectin and other fibers tend to settle at the bottom of the bottle and do not disappear during the acetic fermentation. However, a lot of people get a false impression of the amounts. The content of vitamin C and fiber in cider vinegar cannot be higher than in the apple.

USE IN HERBAL MEDICINE: Apple cider vinegar has experienced a renaissance. It is believed to be helpful to weight loss. However, you cannot lose weight overnight or within 14 days. Therefore, the connection between apple cider vinegar and losing weight is a bit questionable. The acid that is taken in through the mouth mucosa is supposed to block hormones that otherwise encourage the intake of carbohydrates. Other theories claiming that a more intense intestinal peristalsis (rhythmic movement of the intestine) reduce fat absorption or that better protein intake from food makes you slim have remained controversial in the eyes of modern nutrition and medicine. Although the theory is not convincing, a lot of people have lost weight by using the apple cider vinegar diet.

APPLE CIDER VINEGAR DIET

What is special about the apple cider vinegar diet is the fact that regular consumption of apple cider vinegar will satisfy your appetite for sweets and increase your appetite for vegetables and grains. But generally speaking, the only way to lose weight is to reduce the amount of sugar and fat you consume.

Instructions:
• Drink 1 glass of water mixed with 1 teaspoon of apple cider vinegar every morning.
• Be sure to eat 5 meals a day at regular times. Yogurt also counts as a meal. Before each meal drink 1 glass of water mixed with 1 teaspoon of apple cider vinegar. It reduces the appetite.
• Plan your meals. Cook light dishes and use little sugar. A cook book with nutritional recipes can help you.

A word of warning:
Many people also turn to industrially processed apple cider vinegar drinks. But this type of product is not always suitable for losing weight because some of them are sweetened with honey, buckthorn or fruit puree which means that many apple cider vinegar drinks supply undesired calories. Therefore, if your daily consumption is more than 1 bottle, you can expect to gain weight.

IN COOKING

TASTE:

Apple cider vinegar has a mildly sour and fruity taste. The quality and production method will influence the apple flavor of the resulting vinegar. The higher the quality of production, the more flavorful the vinegar.

USE:

Apple cider vinegar is a suitable seasoning for salads, vegetable dishes and chutneys. It goes particularly well with sour pickled pumpkin.

PURCHASE /STORAGE:

You will find apple cider vinegar in every well-stocked supermarket, health food shop, drugstore and pharmacy. Specialties, such as apple cider vinegar made with a particular type of apple, are available in specialty stores that sell oil and vinegar.

You should store apple cider vinegar in a dark area and keep it hermetically sealed. Direct sunshine is not harmful to the vinegar itself, but it destroys the vitamin C contained in the vinegar.

WARNING

Do not prepare an elixir with apple cider vinegar without watering down the vinegar. Undiluted vinegar is harmful because of its tendency to burn. The feeling is comparable sunburnt skin.

COOKING TIPS:

Apple cider vinegar goes very well with nut oils. Sickly sweet fruit puree or fruit sauce can be improved by adding some apple cider vinegar.

Apple cheese salad

INGREDIENTS: 4 tablespoons salad cream or mayonnaise • ½ cup sour cream • juice from ½ lemon• 2 tablespoons apple cider vinegar • freshly ground black pepper • salt • sugar • 1 tablespoon chopped dill • ½ lb sliced cheese • 1 lb red apples • ½ cup walnuts

PREPARATION: To make the dressing, mix the salad cream, sour cream, lemon juice, vinegar, pepper, salt, sugar and dill in a bowl. Slice the cheese into coarse, half inch cubes. Wash the apples thoroughly, quarter and remove the cores. Slice the quartered apples finely. Mix the cheese cubes and apple slices carefully in a bowl. Add chopped walnuts to the apple and cheese mixture. Serve the salad dressing in a separate bowl.

Fine apple jelly

INGREDIENTS: 2 lbs mildly sour apples • 2 tablespoons apple cider vinegar •skin and juice from 1 lemon• 2 lbs sugar • ½ bottle liquid gelatin

PREPARATION: Peel the apples, quarter and remove the cores. Set the apple skin and seeds aside. Mix the water and vinegar in a bowl and add the apple pieces. Heat half a cup of water in a pot and boil the apple skin and cores for 20 minutes until they are soft. Take the pot off the stove and pass the apple mixture through a sieve. Measure half a cup of sieved apples and put into a large pot. Add the lemon peel, juice and sugar and mix thoroughly. Let the mixture boil. Add the apple cubes and boil until they are soft, but not falling apart. Stir in the gelatin, let it boil for a short time and take the pot off the stove. Fill the jars with the hot jelly and seal properly. Keep in a cool place and consume within 1 week after opening.

Fruit vinegar

BASIC INGREDIENTS: Fruit vinegar is a general term for vinegars made with fresh fruit or fruit juice. The following types of fruit are suitable: any garden berries, apples, pears, plums, apricots, peaches and quinces. Exotic fruit, such as pineapple or bananas, can be used for the production of fruit vinegar as well. An exception is citrus fruit. So far, the fermentation of oranges, lemons, limes and grapefruit has not been successful. It is possible that the acetic acid bacteria do not like the high citric acid content.

ORIGIN OF THE BASIC INGREDIENTS: Depending on the type of fruit, the primary ingredients can come from anywhere. In general, particular vinegars are made from the local produce grown in a given country.

CHARACTERISTICS OF THE BASIC INGREDIENTS: Apart from apple cider vinegar, (which we discuss elsewhere,) pure fruit vinegars are made in naturally small quantities. To make high quality vinegar from fruit, the fruit should be overripe, but not spoiled. Juice is extracted from the fruit and yeast cultures are added to make fruit sugar ferment to alcohol. Then, acetic acid bacteria are added to the fruit wine and raw vinegar is made. Some fruit vinegars are allowed to age so that the pulp and acetic acid bacteria can settle.

DIFFERENT VARIETIES: Most fruit vinegars are made from only one type of fruit, or only pomes, such as pears and apples, or only berries, including raspberries and blackberries, fermented together. A lot of fruit juices are sweetened before alcohol fermentation because the sugar content in the juice is too low. Sugar, maple syrup and honey are used. The latter two sweeteners enhance the taste of the vinegar.

COMPOSITION: Fruit vinegar principally contains at least 5% acid. The remaining alcohol content in prepared fruit vinegar can be up to 0.5%. There are also residual amounts of sugar, flavorings, mineral sediments, trace elements and vitamin C.

Raspberry salad with veal liver

Tip:
It is a great idea to add chicken or turkey breast to the salad.

INGREDIENTS: 1 lb fresh raspberries • 2 tablespoons raspberry vinegar • 2 tablespoons raspberry liqueur • salt • white pepper • 1 pinch sugar • 6 tablespoons full-cream yogurt • 1 small head iceberg lettuce • 1 lb fresh veal liver • 2–3 tablespoons butter • 1 bunch tarragon

PREPARATION: Wash the raspberries and let them drain well. Do not rinse in running water. Make purée from the one quarter of the raspberries and mix with raspberry vinegar and liqueur. Season the purée with salt, pepper and sugar. When finished, stir in the yogurt and allow too sit. Wash and trim the iceberg lettuce. Wash the leaves separately, shake well to dry and tear into bite-size pieces. Wash the slices of veal liver, dry and remove the skin, veins and fat. Melt the butter in a large pan over medium heat and fry the veal liver for 3 to 4 minutes on each side. Add salt and pepper. Remove the meat and let it cool. Then cut it into strips. Rinse the tarragon in cold water, shake to dry and mince. Mix up to 1 tablespoon of terragon in a large salad bowl with the iceberg lettuce, raspberries and liver strips. Pour the raspberry dressing carefully on the salad and sprinkle with the remaining terragon.

IN COOKING

TASTE:

Good quality fruit vinegars, like fruit brandies, are recognizable by their fruit flavor. Fruity and mildly sour vinegar is the masterwork of vinegar producers.

USE:

Depending on your personal taste, you can put fruit vinegars on salads and in warm sauces. Another specialty is a dark sauce for game flavored with plum or quince vinegar. If you like experimenting with cooking, you can also put a few drops of high-quality fruit vinegar on vanilla ice cream or use it to season fruit salad.

PURCHASE/STORAGE:

Fruit vinegars are available in specialty stores that sell oil and vinegar. But look at the label carefully. A lot of products that appear to be fruit vinegars at first glance are vinegars that have been flavored with fruits, fruit flavors, fruit puree or fruit leaves. They are not fruit vinegars. If it lists distilled vinegar or wine vinegar as the primary ingredient, it is definitely a vinegar with flavor additives. Such vinegars are cheaper because they are easier to produce.

COOKING TIPS

You should buy fruit vinegars in small bottles because they can be used sparingly. Like other vinegars, they have an unlimited shelf life if sealed and stored in a dark place.

Vegetable vinegar

BASIC INGREDIENTS: Vinegar can also be made from vegetables such as beets, asparagus, tomatoes, carrots or cucumbers.

CHARACTERISTICS OF THE BASIC INGREDIENTS: The production of vegetable vinegar is a demanding process and a vinegar master must be assiduous as well as meticulous. Vegetables are known for their low caloric and sugar content. The sugar content, which yeast bacteria need to make vegetables ferment into alcohol, is therefore limited and is bound in the form of carbohydrate molecules. To produce a wine-like drink, vegetables must be pressed into juice and then preserved so that the carbohydrates are highly concentrated. This process results in a particular type of balsamic vinegar. By adding yeast, an alcoholic liquid will hopefully be formed. However, if the alcohol content is insufficient, the vinegar maker must add some farmer's alcohol himself and leave the mixture to ferment into vinegar using the acetate method. Simple, right? Not really! The vinegar master must perfect the vinegar blend so that the bacteria thrive in the alcoholic vegetable juice and a flavored vinegar is produced. This extra pure vinegar must be left to sit longer in high-grade steel or plastic tanks so that new flavors can be added. Afterwards, it is poured into bottles, and a particular rarity is born.

HISTORY: In the *Wüstenfeld*, the bible of vinegar producers published in the 1930's, you will learn that vegetable vinegar is not just a passing fancy. In the past, people tried not to waste and it was common to produce vinegar from the extra vegetables, such as cucumbers or beets, from an unusually large crop.

DIFFERENT VARIETIES: There are no blended vegetable vinegars. Pure vinegars are made from only one type of vegetable. Vegetable vinegars are clear except for carrot and beet vinegars. You do not even need a sensitive nose or palate to recognize the distinctive smells and flavors of the varieties.

COMPOSITION: In principle, vegetable vinegars contain 5% acid, marked on the bottle as with any other vinegar. The remaining alcohol content can be up to 0.5%. In vinegar, there are flavored additives as well as vitamins resistant to heat such as beta-carotene and minerals such as potassium. But vegetable vinegars are not healthy enough to replace vegetable dishes.

TYPES OF VINEGARS AND DISHES: Asparagus vinegar: Thanks to its typical asparagus flavor, it goes well with cold asparagus salad or cold asparagus pâté. Crab cocktail or ragout fin can also be seasoned with it.

Tomato vinegar: This type of vinegar is great with a couple of drops of Aceto Balsamico. It enhances the taste of tomatoes, and it goes very well with cheese salads of any type.

Cucumber vinegar: This vinegar has an extraordinary freshness. It accompanies fish dishes, braised cucumbers and cold cucumber soup very nicely.

Beet vinegar: A type of vinegar that goes well with Slavic cooking. It is used to marinate vegetables and fish.

Carrot vinegar: Be careful, it stains easily! It has a mildly sweet flavor and can be used to season veal liver. A drop of it is great in vegetable cocktails.

IN COOKING

TASTE:

Vegetable vinegar tastes mildly sour and reminiscent of the particular vegetable flavor from which the vinegar was made.

USE:

Vegetable vinegars are primarily used to season dishes with vegetables, particularly the vegetable from which the vinegar was made.

PURCHASE/STORAGE:

Vegetable vinegars are available in delicacy shops or in specialty stores that sell oil and vinegar. They should be stored in the dark and hermetically sealed.

COOKING TIPS:

You can readily mix vegetable vinegar with sherry vinegar or Aceto Balsamico. If you want to use it for salad dressings, vegetable vinegars combine better with plain oils.

Rice vinegar

PRIMARY INGREDIENT: Rice vinegar is made with rice and rice wine.

ORIGIN OF THE BASIC INGREDIENTS: Rice comes from Asia and its cultivation began about 7000 years ago.

CHARACTERISTICS OF THE BASIC INGREDIENTS: Rice si a gramineous plant and it likes wet enviroments. The plant thrives in shallow water. The fields are drained after blossoming, rice pods ripen and when the panicle has turned yellow, it is harvest time. Rice is threshed, dried and processed just like other grains. Fermentation is necessary to produce rice wine. Depending on the production process and storage time, the alcohol content of rice wine ranges between 15% and 20%. It is then combined with acetic acid bacteria using the acetate method, as with wine vinegar. In China and Japan, the surface method is also popular for producing rice vinegar with a dark color caused by long storage. This is significantly stronger than simple rice vinegar and has a woodier flavor.

DIFFERENT VARIETIES: Chinese rice vinegar is divided into three main groups. "Chen-vinegar," translated as "long storage vinegar," fermented mainly from Sorgho rice or millet at high temperatures. This type of rice vinegar is particu-

larly popular in Shanxi province. The second main type of Chinese vinegar is called "Xiang-vinegar," or "flavored vinegar." The eastern Chinese town Zhenjiang is famous for its flavored rice vinegar. The basic ingredient for flavored vinegar is sticky rice left to ferment at low temperatures. Last but not least, there is vinegar made with oat bran left to ferment at moderate temperatures. The most popular vinegar of this type is called Baoning. In addition to the Chinese varieties, every Asian country has its own special rice vinegars. In Japan, rice vinegar is called "Su." Other Japanese rice vinegars, such as Ponza or Pon vinegar, are also well known. Ponza vinegar is made by adding the lime-like Japanese fruit called Dai Dai.

COMPOSITION: Rice vinegar must contain at least 5% acid and the content of the remaining alcohol must be below 0.5%.

USE IN HERBAL MEDICINE: Vinegar is a tried and trusted medication in Asia and especially in Chinese medicine. Chinese doctors have discovered that it strengthens digestion and liver function. In China, rice vinegar is recommended as a particularly efficient agent against dandruff as well as a natural cleanser for the face and body. If you boil bones for soup, you can add vinegar to make the bone minerals, such as calcium and phosphorus, dissolve into the soup better.

A TRENDY DRINK FROM RICE VINEGAR: Rice vinegar is highly esteemed in the Chinese town of Xi'an. It is popular in restaurants, teahouses and even bars. In Xi'an, vinegar is served as a drink almost everywhere. Vinegar is very popular with young people. One of the "hippest" drinks in Xi'an is a mixture of beer, Sprite and vinegar.

In cooking

Taste:

Rice vinegar has an extremely mild taste and a very delicious acidity.

Use:

Su, Japanese rice vinegar, is a seasoning for Sushi. It not only adds flavor to rice, but also sterilizes raw fish. Chinese rice vinegar is added to soups and wok dishes with meat, fish or vegetables. It makes plain-tasting Tofu sour and pickles vegetables, a tradition in Asia.

Purchase/Storage:

Rice vinegar is available in Asian shops. Although it has been transported a long way, it is among the cheaper vinegars. It should be well-sealed and stored in a dark place.

Cooking tips:

If you do not have rice vinegar on hand, you can use sherry vinegar instead. Instead of rice vinegar, you may find vinegar-soy sauce powder in Asian shops that can be dissolved in water. It is considered an expensive makeshift solution that should be used only if you cannot buy rice vinegar.

Beef with mushrooms

INGREDIENTS FOR 2 PEOPLE: ½ lb beef • 1 tablespoon Marsala wine • 3 tablespoons soy sauce • 3 tablespoons rice vinegar • 1 teaspoon starch • 1 small piece fresh ginger root • 1 clove garlic • 2 small onions • 4 ounces mushrooms • salt • freshly ground pepper • 1 teaspoon sesame seeds

PREPARATION: Cut the beef into thin strips. Mix the Marsala wine, soy sauce, rice vinegar and starch in a small bowl, pour it onto the meat and marinate for 30 minutes. Peel and mince the ginger. Peel and thinly slice the garlic and onions. Prepare the mushrooms, rub them with coarse paper towels and divide into quarters. Heat a pan without oil, take the beef out of the marinade, and sear for about 3 minutes at a high temperature. Put the marinade aside. Season with ginger, garlic, onions and mushrooms and boil for 3 minutes. Add salt and pepper. Lightly brown the sesame seeds in a small pan without oil. Put the meat and sauce on two plates, sprinkle with sesame seeds and serve with rice.

Sweet and sour chicken soup

INGREDIENTS: 6 dried Chinese mushrooms • 2 oz tofu
• 2 carrots • 2 shallots • ½ lb chicken breast • 1 teaspoon
rice wine • salt • freshly ground white pepper • 1 teaspoon soy sauce • 2½ tablespoons starch • 1 teaspoon
peanut oil • 2 cups chicken broth • 1 tablespoon tomato
puree • 1 tablespoon rice vinegar • 1 teaspoon sugar
• 1 teaspoon Sambal Oelek • 2 oz soy sprouts • 2 oz
watercress

PREPARATION: Soak the mushrooms in water for
about 1 hour. Cut the tofu into cubes, prepare the
mushrooms, carrots and sprouts and cut them into
thin strips. Cut the chicken breast into thin strips.
Make a marinade from the rice wine, salt, pepper,
soy sauce, ½ tablespoon of starch and peanut oil.
Let the meat marinate in the sauce for 30 minutes.
Heat the chicken broth, and add the tomato puree,
vinegar, sugar and Sambal Oelek to flavor it. Add
the soy sprouts and carrots, boil about 5 minutes,
add the mushrooms, shallots and tofu cubes to the
broth and boil about 3 minutes. Whip the remaining
starch with 2 tablespoons of cold water and add to the
chicken soup while stirring, bring to a boil and add the
chicken meat. Put it in the sauce for a couple of minutes
until cooked. Wash and chop the watercress. Pour the
soup into small bowls and sprinkle with watercress.

Raisin vinegar

BASIC INGREDIENTS: Raisins are essential for making raisin vinegar. Honey vinegar and vinegars made with dates and figs are produced in a similar manner, so they will be discussed in this chapter as well.

ORIGIN OF THE BASIC INGREDIENTS: The process of drying grapes and other fruits is older than the production of wine or vinegar. It is one of the oldest preserving methods in history, which our ancestors watched occur naturally before they completely understood the process themselves.

CHARACTERISTICS OF THE BASIC INGREDIENTS: The grapes, dried on mats, are boiled and pressed. A very sweet mixture is formed and separated from the grapes. By adding wine yeast, sweet wine is made. In the second stage, the sweet wine is left to oxidize into vinegar. In addition to the acetate method, raisin vinegar is also produced domestically in homes in Turkey, Greece, Algeria, Morocco and Spain. The vinegar is stored in wooden barrels for a long time and, using the traditional process, it acquires a spicy flavor.

HISTORICALLY: Raisin, date and fig vinegars are common in Muslim countries around the Mediterranean. Since

drinking alcohol is banned in the Koran, wine grapes were historically grown only for trade. A large quantity of the grape hervest was dried and consumed as raisins. It does not take much effort to make vinegar from raisins.

DIFFERENT VARIETIES: The production processes of date and fig vinegar are identical. The vinegars are similar in their flavor as well.

COMPOSITION: Raisin vinegar contains at least 5% acid and the content of the remaining alcohol is below 0.5%. Like date and fig vinegar, this type of vinegar has a very high sugar and potassium content.

MEAD VINEGAR

Honey or mead vinegar is still made traditionally in Provence. However, it has been rediscovered by many artisan vinegar producers. Until the Middle Ages, it was the most widely used vinegar in Europe. It was made virtually by accident from mead that was stored for a long time. Mead was the most popular drink of the early Middle Ages. The increase in the variety of grains and the rise of beer production caused mead to became less popular. If you buy honey vinegar today, it is often made from high quality honey such as acacia, sweet chestnut and clover honey. Honey is liquefied, fermented and oxidized. High quality honey vinegar is mildly sour and although it keeps the flavor of its original source, it is not terribly sweet.

IN COOKING

TASTE:
Vinegars made with raisins, dates and figs have a strong fruit flavor. You can taste the delightful aromas of the fruit.

USE:
Vinegars made with raisins, dates and figs are particularly used in oriental cooking. Couscous sprinkled with raisin vinegar charms eaters in the fairyland of The Arabian Nights. The flavor of the vinegar also goes well with oriental lamb or poultry dishes.

PURCHASE/STORAGE:
You should certainly bring this vinegar back with you from your vacation in the Mediterranean because it is available only in specialty shops or stores that sell oil and vinegar. Buy raisin, date and fig vinegar only in small bottles because they should be used sparingly. You should store these vinegars sealed and in a cool, dark place so that they will keep their full flavor for a long time.

COOKING TIPS:
Vinegars made with raisins, dates and figs go particularly well with nut oils.

Arabian rice

INGREDIENTS: 2 tablespoons butter • 2 teaspoons curry • ½ cup long grain rice • 2 cups chicken broth • ½ cup raisins • 1 green pepper • salt • 2 bananas • 3½ tablespoons peanuts • raisin vinegar

PREPARATION: Heat 1 tablespoon of butter in a pot with curry. Add rice and heat until glazed. Pour chicken broth on it and boil. Then lower the temperature and finish boiling in a covered pot. Heat the raisins in a little water, wash the pepper, slice it into quarters, remove the seeds and dice. Mix the drained raisins with the pepper and serve the rice. Salt to taste. Peel and slice the bananas. Chop the nuts and simmer both the banana and the nuts in the remaining butter and salt. Put the rice into a preheated bowl and garnish with the bananas and nuts. Sprinkle carefully with raisin vinegar. It complements lamb gigot or grilled chicken nicely.

Rhine roast sirloin

INGREDIENTS FOR MARINADE: 1 cup red wine • ½ cup raisin vinegar • ½ cup red wine vinegar • 1 cup water • 1 bunch soup greens, peeled and diced • 2 onions, diced • 1 bay leaf • 4 juniper berries, crushed • 2 cloves • 1 tablespoon peppercorns • 1 teaspoon mustard seeds. For the Roast: 2 lb beef from the leg • salt • ground pepper • 3 tablespoons oil • 1 onion, diced • ½ cup raisins • 2 tablespoons almond • 1 tablespoon light molasses • ginger • 2–3 tablespoons butter

PREPARATION: Boil the ingredients for the marinade and let cool. Rinse the meat, drain, dry and put in a bowl. Pour the marinade on it. The meat must be covered with the liquid, which means that it may need to be turned. Let stand for 7 days. Take the meat out of the marinade and rub both sides with salt and pepper. Pour the marinade through a sieve and heat. Sear the meat in oil, add 1 cup of the marinade, onion, cover with a lid and heat for 15 minutes. Turn the roast, add more marinade and baste every 30 minutes. Pour a little marinade gravy on the raisins and allow to swell. After 2 hours, take the roast out, strain the juices, briefly boil, add the raisins, almonds, light molasses, grated ginger and butter. Then season with raisin vinegar.

> **Tip**
>
> The German-Turkish friendship allows you to top off your Rhine roast sirloin with raisin vinegar. You will be impressed with how well both traditional products from these two different cultures go together.

Whey vinegar

BASIC INGREDIENTS: Whey vinegar, also called "Lacto-vinegar," or milk vinegar, is made with concentrated whey.

ORIGIN OF THE BASIC INGREDIENTS: Whey is a secondary product formed during the production of cheese and cottage cheese.

CHARACTERISTICS OF THE BASIC INGREDIENTS: Whey is a whitish, thick liquid. In addition to potassium, calcium, magnesium and phosphorus, it also contains vitamins B1, B2, B6 and B12 as well as lactose (milk sugar), lactic acid and a little fat. The lactose content is too low for whey to ferment directly to alcohol. For this reason, whey is first thickened in a vaporizer until it is 2.5 times thicker. Then it is fermented with lactic acid and heated again to release some of the proteins. Thanks to lactic yeasts, lactose is transformed to alcohol just as in classic vinegar production. The lactic mash is purified and filtered. Then, it is put into acetate, infused with the acetic acid bacteria culture and acetic acid is produced from the alcohol.

SOURCE OF WHEY VINEGARS: Whey vinegar is a Swiss specialty that is not even always available in Switzerland. At the present time, it is also produced under license in France and Austria.

HISTORY: In 1914, the Swiss vinegar producer I. Bourgeois got an order from a French dairy to make vinegar from whey. He was successful and we enjoy this unusual product to this day.

COMPOSITION: Whey vinegar contains acetic acid, lactic acid, and acetic acid, the latter of which is most prevalent. The remaining content of lactose is strictly controlled. Compared to other vinegars, whey vinegar is rich in vitamin B2. Whey vinegar also contains valuable proteins not present in other vinegars.

HEALTH EVALUATION: Internal use: The acidity of whey vinegar is clearly lower than that of wine or alcohol vinegar which is why it is digested better by people suffering from irritated stomach mucosa, gastric and duodenum ulcers or general inflammation of the digestive tract. The lactic acid in this uncommon vinegar has a regulating effect on micro-organisms in the large intestine. However, regular use of whey vinegar is necessary for tangible results.

EXTERNAL USE: Inflammation of the vagina caused by the vaginal fungus "candida albicans" can be soothed by a bath with some whey vinegar added. To get rid of unpleasant itching during the day, you can put a few drops of whey vinegar on a sanitary napkin.

MOLKOSAN – AN ALTERNATIVE TO WHEY VINEGAR: Molkosan is not the same as whey vinegar. It is a vinegar substitute and can be used in cooking like whey vinegar. It is a fermented whey concentrate free of acetic acid and containing lactic acid in a concentration of only about 7 – 8%.

It can be used in salad dressings instead of vinegar, and herb cottage cheese can be seasoned quite well with it. After opening the bottle, it should be stored in a cool place. Finicky eaters use Molkosan instead of vinegar for seasoning. The theory about combined diets says that a higher consumption of vinegar can make the body fluids too sour. Some people believe this can be avoided by using Molkosan as a vinegar substitute.

IN COOKING

TASTE:
Whey vinegar has a milder flavor than any other vinegar.

USE:
In cooking, whey vinegar can be used like white wine vinegar. It is a favorite of people with stomachs sensitive to acidity.

PURCHASE / STORAGE:
You can buy this vinegar in Switzerland yourself or have your friends bring it back for you after their vacations in Switzerland. But it is a rarity even in Switzerland and you are lucky to find it in a health food shop. Because of its low acidity, whey vinegar is perishable and should therefore be kept refrigerated after opening.

COOKING TIPS:
Whey vinegar can be added to both sweet and spicy dishes made with cottage cheese.
If cheese cubes do not melt thoroughly in cheese fondue or cheese sauce, add one spoonful of whey vinegar.

WHEY VINEGAR ELIXIR

If you want to try an elixir with whey vinegar, drink a glass of water with one teaspoon of whey vinegar every morning on an empty stomach. Drinking the elixir regularly has a regulating effect on the intestines. Problems such as irregular bowel movements or constipation can be improved this way.

What is each type of vinegar suitable for?

	Soup	Sauce/Dip	Salad	Raw vegetables	Mushrooms	Smoked meat
Aceto Balsamico	●		●	●	●	
Apple cider vinegar		●	●			
Beer vinegar	●					
Distilled vinegar	●	●	●			
Champagne vinegar	●	●	●			
Cucumber vinegar	●		●	●		
Raspberry vinegar	●	●	●			
Currant vinegar	●	●	●			
Herb vinegar	●	●	●	●	●	
Malt vinegar						
Whey vinegar		●				
Plum vinegar			●			
Rice vinegar	●	●				
Rose vinegar	●	●	●			
Raisin vinegar	●	●	●			
Red wine vinegar				●	●	●
Sherry vinegar	●	●	●	●	●	
Tomato vinegar	●	●	●	●	●	
White wine vinegar	●	●	●	●	●	●
Whiskey vinegar					●	●

Eintopf made with legumes	Beef	Veal	Pork	Lamb	Poultry	Venison/Game	Fish	Dessert	Hard cheese	Cottage cheese	Blue cheese
	●	●	●	●	●	●		●			
					●	●				●	
			●				●				●
●	●	●	●	●	●	●					
		●			●		●	●		●	
							●			●	
				●	●	●		●	●	●	●
				●	●	●		●	●		●
●	●	●	●	●	●	●	●		●	●	
	●	●	●	●	●	●					
									●	●	
	●	●		●	●	●		●		●	●
●		●					●				
				●	●			●		●	
	●			●	●						●
	●	●		●		●			●		
	●	●	●	●	●	●		●		●	●
		●	●		●						
	●					●		●			
●	●	●	●	●	●		●				

Oil

History of cooking oil

SEEDS AND FRUITS CONTAINING OIL – AN IMPORTANT FOOD
FOR PRIMEVAL MAN

While today we frown upon fats and oils, they were
a critical factor in man's survival for a long time. Hunters
and gatherers of the early Stone Age found the first oil
seeds while looking for food. They intuitively realized
how nourishing and nutritious the food was. Seeds such
as sunflower, sesame, poppy and linseeds were popular
since they did not have to be consumed immediately after they had been picked. It was possible to stock up on
them because, when dried in the open air, they could be
stored longer than fruit, roots, fish or meat. Primeval man
could always use them when food ran short.

SESAME – THE OLDEST OIL SUPPLYING CULTIVATED PLANT
ON EARTH

Sesame is among the oldest cultivated plants. It is well-
known that, by the time of the Pharaohs, the Egyptians
used sesame oil in addition to olive and nut oils.
Drawings of the Greek Herodotus (484 - 425 BC) show
that in Babylon, sesame oil was regarded as the main edible oil. It was used as a medication as well. You can

read in the Old Testament how sesame oil was used to heal wounds. By the time of the Trojan War, sesame oil was scented with rose buds. In Homer's Iliad, the beautiful Hera rubbed sesame oil on her body to seduce Paris. Sesame oil was also appreciated as a beauty agent in ancient Rome. The Romans knew that the sesame seed came from India and they were acquainted with its cultivation. Sesame was grown in Sicily until the Middle Ages.

OLIVE OIL – THE OIL OF THE CLASSICAL PERIOD

It is clear that the Cretans ate olives as early as 5000 BC. Documents written by Aristophanes (448 - 380 B. C.) record the Hellenic cooking tradition which used olive oil to prepare vegetable and fish dishes as well as to make pastries and sweets. In ancient Rome, olives and their oil were foods for both the rich and the poor. The cultivated land around Rome did not come close to meeting the Romans' requirements. Therefore, olive oil had to be imported from outlying provinces, mostly from Spain and northern Africa.

The Testaccio Mountain near Ostia recorded how many ships bringing valuable oil to Rome were needed: it is simply covered with shards from broken jars used for oil.

An important center of the olive trade was the Minoan island of Crete. In Zakros, 3,500-year-old earthen jars con-

taining tablets the about olives were discovered. In the southern Peloponnesian town of Pylos, 51 earthen tablets were found with information about receivers and destinations of oil supplies as well as the quality and quantity of oil. The Greeks tried to expand the cultivation of olive trees, particularly to arid climates in Asia Minor, southern Italy, Sicily, southern France and northern Africa. The Romans struggled to raise olives throughout the Mediterranean area, including Spain. After the decline of Carthage, their culture expanded and trade increased. Thanks to the oil trade, Roman colonial rulers became wealthy and Italy gained a dominant position.

Linseed oil – the oil of the German Middle Ages

In the year 1,100, the monk Theophilus described how oil was made from linseeds. Charlemagne and German emperors and kings supported flax cultivation in central Europe. However, the production of oil played a secondary role. Flax was the most important basic ingredient for the production of linen until the 20th century. The wealthy Fugger family became rich thanks to the linen trade. The linen industry flourished in the 15th and 16th centuries. The cultivation of flax particularly increased in Silesia, Lusatia, the Baltic provinces, Westphalia and Schwarzwald, which may explain why linseed oil, cottage cheese and boiled potatoes is a typical dish of Silesia today. You can find it in places where flax has been raised.

LEONARDO DA VINCI MADE DESIGNS FOR OIL PRESSING

Leonardo da Vinci was not the first man to think about the optimal yield of oil factories. Innovations such as lever and compress presses, oscillators and grinding mills already existed in the Classical Period. The artist was concerned with the further development of professional tools. His invention of a more effective olive oil press was not easy for people to obtain at that time because they had little money to invest. Therefore, it took more time before the technique of oil pressing was improved.

Oil was not only pressed by people; animals, such as oxen, donkeys, horses and even dogs were used to mill grains. Making use of their strength, people and animals moved the heavy iron or stone wheels to grind oil seeds. Oil was then pressed from the crushed raw material with a screw press. The most important technological developments for the oil industry were water mills, the lever drive and windmills.

Oil miller – an uncommon craft

The work of a miller is associated with grinding grains to flour. But there are also oil producers who grind seeds from oil plants. According to statistics, in the year 1813, there were 2,828 simple grinding mills with hand and pedal drives in Germany and 522 mills that used the power of horses, wind or water. Many of them stood still during the year and were used only after the harvest. A large oil mill of that time produced about 310 lbs of oil per year. Remember that at the time, oil was used for light as well.

Steam engine – the beginning of industrial oil production

The invention of the steam engine and the hydraulic press created the necessary conditions for production in large quantities. Demand for oil as grease particularly increased with the simultaneous development of railroads. Although oil played a secondary role as food in Germany, margarine was invented in 1869 by Hippolytus Mège-Mouriès and the first large margarine-producing factory was founded in Kleve in 1888. However, butter, lard and cooking fat remained the most important fats in people's diets. The growth of the population in the industrial age and the rise of the megalopolis resulted in a slightly increased demand for margarine, which in addition to vegetable fat, consisted predominantly of suet.

EDIBLE OIL – AN INDISPENSABLE PART OF MODERN NUTRITION

During the war and pre-war eras, margarine and vegetable oils competed against cheap fats. During the 1980s, a margarine-butter war was waged between doctors and scientists concerned about nutrition. But they are all united today: vegetable oils are an important part of a balanced diet. An increasing awareness of health among German people led to a bigger demand for oil. The variety of oils has never been as diverse as it is today. There is still much that we do not know about the nutritional differences between the edible oils.

Production of oil

In addition to the traditional processes of oil production, most consumed oil is produced industrially at present. Technical developments have significantly improved the oil yield of plants through a combination of improved custom processes and modern industrial methods.

DELIVERY OF OIL SEEDS

Most oil, including rapeseed oil, is imported. Oil production factories are, therefore, usually located close to seaports or inland ports. First, the oily product is cleaned by strong magnets that collect any remaining metal. Various filters remove sand, stones, wood or other types of dirt.

SHELLING AND PRESSING OF THE BASIC INGREDIENTS

The basic ingredients with shells, such as sunflower seeds or nuts, must be shelled. There are special shelling machines which separate the meat from the shell.

The conventional process of oil pressing

After pressing the basic ingredients, which contain more than 30% oil, steaming or roasting takes place on heated surfaces. The cells are opened by heat and moisture so that the oil can be extracted more easily and pressed. There are various pressing methods which make use of lower or higher pressure in order to press oil from the basic ingredients. One example is a large, spiral press surrounded by metal grates from which oil flows sideways. The "oil cake" is removed from the spiral and is also processed by the grinding mill to obtain edible oil. With this method, extracted oils are not yet edible. They contain a lot of unpleasant, bad-smelling and irritating substances as well as free fatty acids. To make the oil edible, it must be refined.

Extraction for basic ingredients with a lower fat content

The basic ingredients, soybeans, for example, which contain less than 20% oil as well as the oil pressed from seeds, undergo a special extraction process. In the counterflow process, while the fat is extracted, a dissolving agent

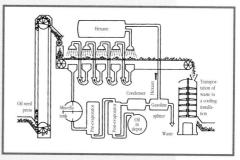

called hexane is added to the basic ingredients to achieve an optimal yield of oil. A substance which millers call "Miscella" containing fat and solvents, drains away. This oily blend is de-aerated thermally, meaning the blend is heated to a temperature of about 140°F and hexane is separated from the oil just as in alcohol distillation.

REFINEMENT

The elimination of the pulp follows. Vegetable traces, dregs and phosphorus lipids are separated. Undesired substances are removed with watered down brine and acid dilutions. Oil is de-acidified, so that fatty acids, which have an unpleasant taste, are removed. The de-acidification is carried out by adding sodium lye, which allows soaps to form from free fatty acids. The soaps are then washed out of the oil with hot water. This stage is followed by bleaching. The oil is heated temperatures between 158° 194°F and kaolin is put into the hot oil. Kaolin absorbs pigments and other undesired things such as heavy metals. The oil is winterized, which means that it is cooled to 32°F to form crystals and filter oot the components with a higher melting point. At the end of the multi-stage process, of oil is deodorized. The fat is subjected to temperatures up to 518° F for a maximum of 30 minutes in a vacuum with steam. This expensive process produces a long-lasting, bland oil of consistent quality. A small amount of vitamin E is produced during the deodorizing process. A long chain of different stages is necessary during the industrial production of oil because an optimal yield needs to be gained from the basic ingredients. Extreme pressing leads to a high proportion of undesirable substances in the semi-finished product which must then be removed from the oil.

COLD PRESSING

During cold pressing, oil seeds are not treated with heat. A high enough pressure should be used so that the draining oil does not reach temperatures higher than 104°F. The heat is formed by great pressure. It makes oils, as well as other useful and less useful secondary materials soluble in oils, drain from from plant cells better. For this reason, the same amount of oil cannot be pressed from each fruit by cold pressing. Only the simpler, more usable oils can be obtained. Cold pressed oils must not be refined. After they have been pressed, they should be filtered and dried. For the oil miller, the term dried means that only a minimum amount of natural water is extracted from the oil. There is no need to use an expensive refining process because, with regard to its ingredients, the cold pressed oil is basically pure.

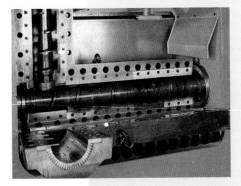

EVALUATION OF COLD PRESSED AND REFINED OILS

Cold pressed oil is also a natural and rare product. To produce the same amount of cold pressed oil, considerably more basic ingredients are needed than for the same amount of refined oil. The shelf life of cold pressed oils is usually shorter than that of oils produced industrially. The range of flavors and aromas is significantly more diverse and cold pressed oils have more unique flavors. The vitamin E content of, which protects the body against undesired metabolic processes caused by stress, is usually higher as well as the proportion of accompanying substances with health benefits. The fatty acid content is not essentially different between refined and cold pressed oils.

SEDIMENTS IN COLD PRESSED OILS

Cold pressed oil can contain sediments if it is not filtered. They settle at the bottom of the bottle. Such oil is not accepted by many consumers and is regarded as impure. However, gourmets specifically prefer such oils. Oil producers recommend shaking the bottle before using oils with sediments because there is extremely intense flavor in the sediments.

Oil & its ingredients

At first glance, oil is a yellow fluid. Consumers hear many confusing, and sometimes incomprehensible, advice about oil: "Olive oil is particularly healthy!" or "Cold pressed oils should be used only in cold cooking!" Such statements have been taken out of context. The chaos can only be resolved if you learn about the chemistry of edible oils.

WHAT DOES EVERY TYPE OF OIL HAVE IN COMMON?

Edible oils consist of 99.9% fat. All fats have a similar structure. A fat molecule consists of one unit of glycerin and three units of fatty acids. The molecule of glycerin has an identical structure for each fat molecule. It is characterized in an isolated state and has three alcohol OH groups. These groups bond to the molecules of fatty acids. All fatty acids have the OOH group typical of organic acids. These different groups are bonded to each other. Chemists call the process: the first formation. A molecule of glycerin bonds to three fatty acids at a time and water is formed. Fatty acids consist of a longer or shorter chain of carbons. In each chain, there are fatty acids naturally present which consist of an even number of carbon atoms. They are broken down by the human body.

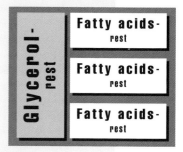

WHAT MAKES OILS DIFFERENT?

A critical factor is that different fatty acids have different structures. There are short, medium and long fatty acid chains. The longer a fatty acid chain, the lower the melting point. All types of vegetable oil have long-chain fatty acids and, therefore, they are fluid at room temperature. Furthermore, the melting point depends on the type of fatty acid. Fatty acids can be roughly classified as unsaturated and saturated fatty acids. The more unsaturated bonds, the lower the melting point. The word 'unsaturated' means that the carbon chain forms double bonds. The unsaturated fatty acids are further divided into simple and polyunsaturated fatty acids. Oleic acid is among the simple, unsaturated fatty acids and linoleic and linolenic acid are among the polyunsaturated fatty acids.

Although Omega-6- and Omega-3-fatty acids are mentioned, it is poly-unsaturated fatty acids that are described this way. Dieticians set the description Omega and the number where there is a double bond in the carbon chain. It is counted from the free side to the molecule of glycerin. That means that an Omega-6 fatty acid has the first double bond between the sixth and seventh atom of

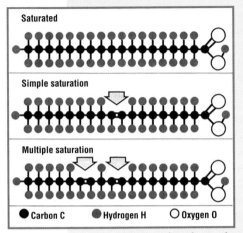

Saturated

Simple saturation

Multiple saturation

● Carbon C ● Hydrogen H ○ Oxygen O

carbon. The human body can produce fatty acids, but is not able to form Omega-3 and Omega-6 fatty acids. These fats are important for nutrition.

UNSATURATED FATTY ACIDS SEEK HYDROGEN

Saturated fatty acids are chemically more consistent. The polyunsaturated fatty acids attempt to break up the double bonds. For this purpose, two atoms of hydrogen per double bond are necessary. The more double bonds a fatty acid has, the more difficult it is to break them up. For example, they are only activated at higher temperatures. At the same time, they take hydrogen away from weaker molecules and free radicals can form. These free radicals can cause cancer. For this reason, fats with a high proportion of triple unsaturated fatty acids should not be heated and fats with a high proportion of double unsaturated fatty acids should not be heated repeatedly because there is a risk that free radicals will be formed. Most oils with a high proportion of unsaturated fatty acids contain vitamin E, which has an antioxidant effect and blocks the formation of free radicals.

FREE FATTY ACIDS

The term free fatty acids means fatty acids that have not been bonded to glycerin. The oxidation changes proceed faster due to light and high temperatures and they react to the oxygen in the air and become rotten. Where refined oils are concerned, the free fatty acids are eliminated during the refining processes. Thus they usually keep longer and are more stable when heated.

TRANSFORMED FATTY ACIDS

Transformed fatty acids do not occur naturally in vegetables. They can be formed at high temperatures, particularly during the solidification of oils with a high proportion of polyunsaturated fatty acids, which makes margarine. The formation of these fatty acids can also occur during refinement and is dependent on temperature. Transformed fatty acids are considered a risk factor for heart and circulatory diseases. Dieticians have agreed that the main sources of transformed fatty acids are solidified margarine, baking fats, and snacks and sweets, all of which should be avoided. The consumption of refined, edible oils is not considered a problem.

Vitamin E

All vegetable oils contain vitamin E. Vitamin E is soluble in fat and serves as a natural protection for plants because it protects polyunsaturated fatty acids against oxidation. During refinement, some vitamin E dissolves, but it is often added again later to oils. Therefore, refined oils cannot generally be said to be richer in vitamin E than cold pressed oils.

Oil & health

Fat, with its 9.3 kilocalories per gram, is the most efficient supplier of energy. Obesity is caused by excessive energy production, which means that the energy supplied by the food is higher than the body is able to burn off. A high consumption of fat has generally been regarded as the only cause, or at least the main reason, for weight gain and, therefore, it is thought to be an unhealthy ingredient. The fact that fat contains vitally important fatty acids, such as linoleic and linolenic acids, and that soluble vitamins A, E, D and K can only be absorbed in fat, has been ignored. On the one hand, fat is our body's energy reserve and it assumes important functions in the body. Fatty acids give structure to cell membranes and form a base for hormones. The subcutaneous fatty tissue buffers extreme temperatures and important organs are protected against jolts by surrounding fatty tissue. To eat no fat is as unhealthy as to eat too much fat.

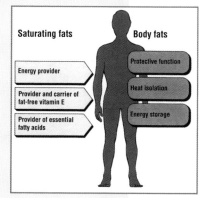

Saturating fats

Energy provider

Provider and carrier of fat-free vitamin E

Provider of essential fatty acids

Body fats

Protective function

Heat isolation

Energy storage

OIL – A PARTICULAR FAT

Vegetable fats in the form of oil have a wide health function. As all vegetable fats are free of cholesterol, they usually have a good range of fatty acids and they contain essential fatty acids as well as vitamin E.

OLEIC ACID REDUCES THE RISK OF HEART ATTACKS

There are simple, unsaturated fatty acids in all vegetable fats. They are fluid at room temperature and somewhat concentrated. The oils with the most oleic acid are olive, rapeseed and almond oil. Scientific studies prove that oleic acid particularly decreases cholesterol level. Blood cholesterol is subdivided into two components: good HDL and bad LDL. The polyunsaturated fatty acids have a similar effect mechanism as the oleic acid. A higher consumption of oil and lower cinsumption of fatty meat products and cheap solidified fats in sweets and snacks decreases the level of the dangerous LDL cholesterol and increases the level of positive HDL cholesterol. Furthermore, the consumption of vegetable oils rich in vitamin E and oleic acid block the undesired oxidation processes which contribute to arteriosclerosis.

Linoleic and Linolenic Acid and Their Roles

Although the effect of linoleic acid against heart and circulatory diseases was exaggerated for a long time, it still plays an important role in nutrition. There is a high content of linoleic acid in wheat germ, corn, thistleseed, sunflower and soy oil. But the need for this fatty acid can also be met by using 2 or 3 spoonfuls a day of all other types of oil. A one-sided, extremely high consumption of these oils with a high proportion of polyunsaturated fatty acids is viewed critically by dieticians today. An excessive supply can influence the oxidation rate of bonds in fatty acids of the tissue and blood in a negative way. Whether or not a person has an increased risk of acquiring an allergy or cancer due to this process is a controversial subject today. Linoleic and linolenic acids are indispensable to the body, promoting supple musculature, such as the heart muscle. They also have an anti-inflammatory effect and contribute to the structure of many hormones.

Vitamin E – a Protection for Plants and Man

Vitamins are vitally important to the human body. The body cannot make them by itself, so we are dependent on our diets to supply necessary vitamins. Basically, there are 13 different vitamins that are important for nutrition. Vitamin E is, along with three other vitamins, soluble in fat and abundant in vegetable oils. Vitamin E plays the same role in oil plants as in the body, working as an antioxidant and warding off undesirable molecules. Whether or not poor intake of this vitamin increases the number of radicals formed and increases the risk of cancer continues to be a controversial subject.

OIL ELIMINATION TREATMENT

The oil treatment, an alternative medicine from Russia, is gaining popularity in the West. Sipping cold pressed oil (traditionally sunflower oil) regularly relieves tooth and headaches as well as stomach and intestinal problems. It also detoxifies the body and generally improves well being. It should be done like this:

- **In the morning, just after getting up, put one teaspoon of cold pressed oil into your mouth and move it with your tongue and cheeks.**
- **Do this for at least 10 minutes and then spit it out. Rinse your mouth thoroughly and brush your teeth.**
- **To be successful, the treatment must be carried out for 4 weeks.**

Oil & external use

Massage with oil for muscle tone

People in classical Greece and Rome knew that stiff muscles, cramps, tension and pain in the joints can be treated with a massage. To perform a proper massage, you need quality oil. There is a large variety of special massage oils mixed with special aromas or herbs. But you can massage the body with common edible oil as well. If you like, you can add an aroma yourself.

By rubbing and kneading, heat is formed. Oil stores this energy very well, and if it is slightly warm, it is absorbed by the skin very quickly. It removes stiffness with a soothing heat and produces a pleasant feeling in the body.

OIL FOR THE SKIN AND HAIR

There are expensive, cosmetic body oils, of course. However, using natural oils for cream is such an old formula that it originated during the time of the pharaohs in ancient Egypt. The pharaohs used the same oil for cooking as they used for greasing their skin and hair. All edible oils contain, in addition to fat, natural vitamin E which enhances the elasticity and resilience of the skin.

Herbs were often added to oil. For example, St. John's wort makes the skin tan nicely while sunbathing. If you are sunburnt, you can cool yourself with olive oil and a few drops of lemon juice. If you prefer flavored oil, you can add any scented, flavored essences that you like. If the oil is heated mildly in warm water, it will be more effective. Usually only dry skin needs oil, but normal skin often has dry, scaly spots. After rubbing in a few drops of oil for a couple of days, the skin will be smooth and soft again. The hair also needs oil, particularly when dry air in buildings damages it. The easiest way is to add some oil to your favorite shampoo and then wash the hair thoroughly. Dull hair will becomes shiny again.

NAILS WILL SHINE AGAIN

If your fingernails are dull and brittle because your hands often come in contact with chemicals, cleaners or other harsh products, you can recover a nice shine and resilience for your nails by putting some oil on a wool pad and rubbing your fingernails with it daily.

OIL AS A BATH INGREDIENT

Some oil in a bubble bath refreshes tired skin. For dry and heavily peeling skin, a bath with sea salt and oil can have a soothing effect. Oil floats on the water surface like specks of fat in soup. For this reason, it is useful to rub the oil in with a sponge. The sponge should be washed after use.

OIL IN AROMATHERAPY

Aromatherapy originated more than 6000 years ago in Egyptian temples. Essential oils, highly efficient vegetable substances, were used to put the pharaohs into a trance and the gods in charitable mood. Essential oils contain the highly concentrated vital energy of plants. They can be used in a flavored bath, relaxing massage oil or in an enchanting room aroma. The oils have a refreshing, focusing or relaxing effect and are used by doctors and healers for treating diseases. A scented oil lamp can work small miracles too. For example, roses work as an antidepressant, oranges have a relaxing effect and box-gum is stimulating.

Oil in the household

OIL HAS MANY USES

Have you ever heard of the man who filled his gas tank with salad oil? I cannot judge whether this is good for your engine, but organic diesel is now available at more and more gas stations. It differs from salad oil in that the diesel molecule is first bonded to glycerin and its three fatty acids. Edible oils can not only be used for cooking, but as a valuable alternative for many household agents too.

Oil can be used to grease a squeaky door, a handle or a bicycle brake. Today, there is a special oil for each type of squeak, but annoying squeaking can be removed with a few drops of edible oil too.

OIL AS A SOLVENT: Price tags are often difficult to remove from the new purchases because the glue remains on the merchandise. The easiest way to remove the remaining glue is to rub the goods with some oil. Of course, this is only possible with products that you can wash with water afterwards, and certainly not textiles!

OIL AS A FURNITURE POLISH: Unsightly stains on polished furniture can be removed with firm, circular rubbing with edible oil. Let the oil soak in for some time and polish later.

OIL IN THE KITCHEN

OIL AS A SEPARATING AGENT:
More damp air than desired
often gets into the deep
freeze or the freezer. Con-
tainers freeze to each other
because the water vapour
coming from the air around
them freezes. This problem
can be avoided if the con-
tainers are brushed with oil.

OIL FOR FRYING: in German
households, little vegetable oil was used 50 years ago.
Margarine and animal fat were typical frying fats. It is still
uncertain if any oil is suitable for frying. In principle,
nearly all oils are heat-resistant if they are not heated be-
yond 320°F for 30 minutes. The higher the proportion of
saturated and unsaturated fatty acids, the more suitable
they are for frying and cooking. There is a widespread,
false opinion that cold pressed oils must not be heated.

OIL AS A PRESERVATIVE: You enjoy foods preserved in oil
from Mediterranean countries without considering the
history of food preservation. Highly perishable vegetables, fish and spices could be kept for a longer period
this way. Fruits and vegetables harvested and gathered in
the summer and and fall could be stored until the fol-

lowing spring. Olive oil used to preserve such treasures could be used a second time for cooking.

MAYONNAISE OIL AND WATER

Mayonnaise is said to have been invented in the capital of Menorca, in Mahón. The duke Richelieu, who expelled the English from the island with French troops in 1756, and subsequently became governor, learned about mayonnaise on the island and took the recipe with him to Paris. However, the French are sure that they invented mayonnaise. It can be said that they have contributed to making the product famous and to its improvement as well. It is not important which nation invented mayonnaise, but a delicious mayonnaise always contains a lot of good oil. You can make mayonnaise yourself as well by combining two or three egg yolks with a little salt in a mixer and adding oil slowly while mixing. You can use oil with natural flavor as well as flavored oils. It depends on how you want your mayonnaise to taste.

WHAT HAPPENS IF OIL BECOMES RANCID?

Rancid oil has changed chemically because it is too old and has been improperly stored, for example, exposed to light, resulting in unpleasant changes of taste and aroma. These hydrolytic processes (reactions with water) release free fatty acids. If there are short or medium chain fatty acids, a soapy residue is formed. Oxidation processes (reactions with oxygen), stimulated by light, heat or metallic elements cause the formation of saturated or unsaturated aldehydes or ketones. Even in small concentrations, the oil is no longer edible. Influenced by enzymes such as lipases or lipoxygenases, free fatty acids and aldehydes and ketones can be formed and they can give a rancid taste to the fat.

How to make flavored oil

You can easily make flavored oils yourself. You can use any plain oil if the flavor of the ingredient is delicate or if its taste can be enjoyed separately. In any case, oil with a unique flavor can also be used if it goes well with the flavor of the ingredient.

THE RIGHT FLAVOR

Suitable ingredients are flavorful foods with relatively low water content. Popular ingredients are herbs, spices and flowers. You should wash them thoroughly so that they are free of dirt and mold. Then they should be dried because the lower the water content is in the oil, the longer its shelf life will be. Onions and garlic, as well as sweet pepper and chili, must be prepared first. Depending on your preference and how you would like the finished product to look, you may chop the herbs or other ingredients. The finer you chop the flavored ingredients, the faster and more intensely the flavor will be formed. Thanks to their light weight, the ingredients will usually float on top of the oil until they become saturated and sink. Therefore, depending on the ingredient and

how intense you would like the flavor to be, you should separate the oil from the flavored ingredients after one or two weeks. If you place more significance on appearance (for example for gifts), you will want to leave the ingredients in bigger pieces that are pleasing to the eyes.

THE OPTIMAL PLACE TO FORM THE FLAVOR

Many people believe that a flavor can be released from a certain ingredient better with the help of sunshine when it is absorbed by the oil. This is false. On the contrary, sun exposure leads to a loss of quality. Flavored oil should always be kept in sealed jars and in dark, cool places both during production and storage later.

Recipes

Chili oil: soy oil, sunflower oil or canola oil; 2 red chili peppers without seeds, chopped finely; 3 finely cut onions; 1 spoonful of pepper.

Removing the spices from the oil after about one week is recommended.

Ginger lemon grass oil: soy oil, sunflower oil or canola oil; 1 piece of ginger (about 1 in long), cut finely; 2 stalks lemon grass, cut finely.

Remove the spices from the oil after about one week.

"Toscana" Oil: olive oil, soy oil, sunflower oil or canola oil; 2 shoots rosemary; 3 shoots thyme; 3 peeled garlic cloves; 5 black peppercorns.

Removing the spices from the oil after about 2 weeks is recommended.

Oil for lovers: soy oil, sunflower oil or canola oil; 2 handfuls rose petals.

It is recommended that you remove the rose petals after about three weeks, otherwise they leave a soapy taste.

Garlic oil: olive oil, sunflower oil or canola oil; 10 garlic cloves, peeled; 20 black peppercorns.

Removing the spices from the oil after about 10 days is recommended.

"FINE HERB" OIL: soy oil, sunflower oil or canola oil; 3 shoots estragon; 6 shoots parsley; ½ bunch of chives; 8 shoots chervil.

You should chop the herbs finely and remove them from the oil after about three weeks.

TRUFFLE OIL: soy oil, sunflower oil or canola oil; 1 walnut-size truffle.

Slice the truffle and remove it from the oil after about 1 month.

"PROVENCE" OIL: soy oil, sunflower oil or canola; 3 shoots thyme; 5 bay leaves; 1 tablespoon dry lavender flowers. It is recommended that you remove the spices after about 1–2 weeks.

MINT OIL: soy oil, sunflower oil or canola oil, 6 sprigs mint, minced.

You should separate the oil and mint leaves after about one week.

The recommended amount is always for 2 cups.

Peanut oil

BASIC INGREDIENTS: 100% peanut oil.

ORIGIN OF THE BASIC INGREDIENTS: The peanut plant comes from Brazil and it is mainly grown in the southern states of the United States, Mexico, western Africa, India and China today. The best quality peanuts come from the United States.

CHARACTERISTICS OF THE BASIC INGREDIENTS: Peanuts come from a shrub in which the blossom shoots bore themselves into the ground after being fertilized. This special process, called "geocarpy" or "underground ripening" by biologists, increases the possibility of successfully developing open-air peanut farming. The fruits mature at a depth of 2 to 3 in. Under the, fragile shell, there are usually two fruits with thin, brown skins. Peanuts are not actually nuts, but belong to the legume family. They are rich in protein, containing about 1 oz of protein per 3 oz of peanuts. The fat content is near 50% and therefore they are extremely useful in the production of edible oil.

FROM HISTORY: Peanuts were grown very early, about 3000 years ago, by Native Americans in South America. Since the discovery of America in the 15th century, peanuts have spread quickly into tropical areas around

the world. Europeans did not pay particular attention to this fruit until the end of the 18th century, although it was described in detail by the Spaniards Oviedo and Monardes in the 16th century. In the middle of the 19th century, an oil producing industry was established in France producing mainly peanut oils. This new industry began by importing from African colonies.

DIFFERENT VARIETIES: In our stores, most peanut oil on sale is refined, but there are also pressed peanut oils. You will find the latter in special shops selling oil and vinegar.

Peanut oil contains arachin, behen and lignoceric acid. These three fatty acids is to ensure that the oil is thick and has a creamy consistency at low temperatures. Peanut butter, which consists of ground peanuts, is gaining more and more favor. In the United States, it replaces butter for breakfast.

COMPOSITION:

19.5% saturated fatty acids: 12% palatic acid, 7.5% stearic acid

37% unsaturated fatty acids: 35% oleic acid

43.5% polyunsaturated fatty acids: 42% linoleic acid

26mg of vitamin E /100ml

DID YOU KNOW ...?

In Switzerland, peanuts are still called Spanish Nuts. In Berlin, the description "Cameroon" has been used since Emperor Wilhelm's time because peanuts were imported from the German colony.

IN COOKING

TASTE:

Refined peanut oil has a neutral flavor. Cold pressed oil, gives you a slight peanut flavor on your tongue.

USE:

Refined peanut oil can be heated to a very high temperature. Therefore, it is suitable for frying, grilling and deep-frying. In cold cooking, it is used in the production of mayonnaise and remoulades.

Cold pressed peanut oils are preferable for salads, not for deep-frying. They are also suitable for roasting meat, particularly poultry, for a short time or for cooking in a wok, particularly if you want to add a nut flavor to a dish.

PURCHASE/STORAGE:

Refined peanut oil is good for about 18 months. The cold pressed oil does not keep as long. Both products are marked with a "best before" date, which you should follow. Peanut oil should be stored in a cool, dark place. It need not stay in the fridge, but should not be exposed to direct sunlight. This shortens its shelf life and the oil becomes rancid more quickly.

Chicken in a peanut crust

Tip
Peanut oil is light yellow and it gets thick in the fridge at temperatures below 46°F.

INGREDIENTS: 1 fresh chicken • 5 tablespoons peanut oil • 2 tablespoons of lemon juice • 3½ oz cornstarch • 1 tablespoon curry powder • a trace of saffron• 1 teaspoon turmeric • freshly ground pepper • 3 tablespoons peanut butter • 2 tablespoons fresh coriander leaves • 2 tablespoons yogurt • 2 eggs • salt • 4 tablespoons coconut milk

PREPARATION: Wash and drain the chicken. Divide it into 8 portions with poultry scissors and put it in a flat baking dish. Mix peanut oil and lemon juice, roll the chicken meat in it and let it sit for about 4 hours. Prepare three mixtures for the panada: mix the cornstarch, curry powder, saffron, turmeric and pepper on a large plate and put it aside. Salt the eggs, whip with the coconut milk and put them on a plate next to the first. Roll the pieces of chicken in the cornstarch mixture, then the peanut oil, then the eggs and, finally, one more time in the cornstarch mixture. Put the chicken in an oiled grill pan with a few drops of peanut oil on it and grill for about 25-30 minutes carefully turning occasionally.

Vegetable kebabs with spicy dip

INGREDIENTS: 2 onions • 2 small zucchini • 2½ oz small mushrooms • 1 red pepper • ½ cup vegetable broth • 2 teaspoons peanut oil • freshly ground pepper • juice from 1 lemon • 2 metal or wooden kebab skewers • 5 tablespoons tomato ketchup • 1 tablespoon light salad cream • 1 garlic clove • ½ bunch coriander • 1 pinch chili powder

PREPARATION: Peel and cut the onions into halves, wash and cut the zucchini into 1 in thick slices. Trim and brush the mushrooms and rub them with a paper towel. Quarter the pepper, wash, and cut it into 1 in strips. Heat the vegetable broth in a flat casserole, add vegetables and simmer covered for 10 minutes. Preheat the oven to a temperature of 338°F. Take out the vegetables, drain, alternate halves of onion, zucchini and whole mushrooms on long metal or wooden skewers and oil. Grill in the oven for 10-15 minutes. Season with freshly ground pepper and sprinkle with lemon juice.

To make the dip, mix tomato ketchup and salad cream. Peel a garlic clove and mince. Wash the coriander, drain and mince. Mix both into the dip. Season the dip with chili powder and serve with the kebobs.

Hazelnut oil

BASIC INGREDIENTS: 100% hazelnut oil.

ORIGIN OF THE BASIC INGREDIENTS: The hazelnut bush has been widespread in Europe and Asia Minor for a long time. Its origin is not precisely known. The main producers of hazelnuts are Turkey, Italy, Spain, the United States and Greece.

CHARACTERISTICS OF THE BASIC INGREDIENTS: The hazelnut bush is monoclinic. Male flowers are long and yellow-and-green catkins that have a slight resemblance to worms. Female flowers are markedly less visible: 8-16 petals always remain close to the bud which protects them a little against frost because they blossom very early depending on the climate conditions between January and March. In the fall, the hazelnuts begin to develop. The nuts, covered with a shell, are coated also with a light green, leafy covering called a cupula. Between 1 and 3 nuts develop from a female bud. The hazelnuts fall out of the leaflike coverings, which decompose slowly. The nuts are dried and shelled. The hazelnut itself is coated with a thin, brown, tight skin, which is removed and the white-and-yellow hazelnut emerges. It contains 60% to 66% fat, which is usually obtained through the cold press process.

From history: Hazelnuts were a common food as far back as the early Stone Age. The hazelnut bush was cultivated in Europe very early.

Different varieties: Hazelnut oil is almost always cold pressed. Refined hazelnut oil is marketed as the best edible oil. However, pay attention to the label. Sometimes mixtures are made by adding expensive nut oils to ordinary, cheap oils and they are not marked clearly. The list of ingredients provides information on whether it is pure oil or a mixture.

COMPOSITION:
8% saturated fatty acids: 6% palmitic acid, 2% stearic acid
78% unsaturated fatty acids: 78% oleic acid
14% polyunsaturated fatty acids: 12% linoleic acid, 2% linolenic acid
35mg vitamin E /100ml

HEALTH EVALUATION: Hazelnut oil has a high proportion of simple unsaturated fatty acids, and therefore, it can be considered rather healthful.

HAZELNUT OIL IN COSMETICS: Hazelnut is, thanks to its light nut aroma, an ideal skin care agent, notably suitable for massage oils and a favorite for basic oils in aromatherapy. Hazelnut oil helps with many skin problems, particularly sensitive or dry skin.

DID YOU KNOW …?

There are many types of hazelnuts. The hazel tree, or Turkish hazel, reaches a height of 66 ft and forms a neat, pyramidal treetop. It is the most cultivated tree in Turkey and the Balkans. Nuts of this type are often cultivated and used as an oil source.

IN COOKING

TASTE:
Hazelnut oil is light yellow, clear and has an intense nut flavor.

USE:
Hazelnut oil cannot be heated to a high temperature and it is therefore primarily suitable for cold cooking. It goes quite well with mildly bitter, green, leafy vegetables such as endives, field lettuce and radicchio. It also works with dressings in salads containing cheese or a lot of fruit. It goes particularly well with grapes, oranges and kiwis so you can use it on desserts and fruit salads, on hot waffles or sprinkled on crepes.

PURCHASE/STORAGE:
Hazelnut oil is only available in specialty or health food stores. It is a rare and expensive edible oil and is only sold in small bottles. It is best to store the oil in a cool, dark place. After opening the bottle, it should be consumed as soon as possible because it becomes rancid quickly.

COOKING TIPS:
Hazelnut oil can be mixed with plain oil in order to dilute the nut flavor.
Store opened bottles of hazelnut oil in the fridge to keep the oil fresh longer.

Cream of asparagus soup with hazelnut oil

Tip
When asparagus is out of season, you can also prepare the soup with cauliflower instead of asparagus using the same method.

INGREDIENTS: 1 lb asparagus • 2 tablespoons butter • 1 spoonful flour • ½ cup milk • 1 ½ cups bouillon • ½ cup light cream • 4 tablespoons grated hazelnuts • salt • black pepper • 1 pinch sugar • 4 tablespoons dry sherry • 4 teaspoons hazelnut oil.

PREPARATION: Peel the asparagus stalks and cut off the tips. Cut the remaining asparagus into 1 in pieces. Melt the butter in a pot and simmer the asparagus, without the tips, in the butter. Sprinkle with flour and simmer a little longer. Dilute with the milk and bouillon and let it cook for 10 minutes. Purée. Add the tips of the as-

paragus and cream and let it all cook for 5 minutes. Roast the grated hazelnut in an oiled pan. Season the soup with salt, pepper, sugar and sherry. Pour into 4 plates, garnish with the grated hazelnuts and sprinkle with oil. If you want to serve it the classic way, replace the hazelnut with cut chives.

Crepes with caramelized peaches

INGREDIENTS: ½ cup milk • 6 tablespoons flour • 1 pinch salt • 3 eggs • 4 tablespoons butter • 2 peaches • 2 tablespoons brown sugar • 2 teaspoons hazelnut oil

PREPARATION: Mix the milk with the flour, salt and eggs to make a smooth batter and let sit for 20 minutes. Bake 8 thin crepes one after the other. Keep adding butter to the pan and fry quickly. Use 4 tablespoons of batter for each crepe and spread evenly. Leave the crepes in the oven heated to 176°F. Wash the peaches, halve them, remove the flesh and cut into thin pieces. Caramelize the remaining butter and sugar and roll the peaches in the caramel. Put 2 crepes and a quater of the caramelized peaches on each plate and sprinkle with hazelnut oil.

Tip
You can use apricots, mangos or strawberries instead of peaches.

Macadamia nut oil

BASIC INGREDIENTS: 100% macadamia nut oil.

ORIGIN OF THE BASIC INGREDIENTS: The Macadamia tree has its origin in the rainforests of Queensland in northern Australia. At present, 40% of the world's macadamia production comes from Australia. The nuts are also grown in Hawaii, Southern Africa, Kenya, Brazil and Costa Rica.

CHARACTERISTICS OF THE BASIC INGREDIENTS: Macadamia nuts have a diameter of 1 in and a hard, brown shell. They look a bit like hazelnuts. They have a slightly sweet taste and the meat is unusually soft. The nuts are the fruit of an evergreen tree with rigid leaves which grows in damp, subtropical climates and reaches a height of between 40 and 50 ft. After about 7 years, the tree bears enough nuts to sell. When it is about 50 years old, it produces between 66 and 88 lbs of nuts per year and will do so for 30 years. The ripe nuts fall off the tree and are gathered with a specially made harvester. Then the nuts are dried, scraped out of their green covering and shelled. Oil is pressed from the meat.

FROM HISTORY: Macadamia nuts were a valuable nutrient for the Australian Aborigines. The Europeans first dis-

covered the tasty nut in 1877. Three years later, the first plantations were established. However, it took more than 100 years before the nut became known outside Australia.

DIFFERENT VARIETIES: As a basic ingredient, macadamia nuts are extremely expensive and only a very small quantity are processed into oil. The oil is produced by the cold-press process.

COMPOSITION:
14% saturated fatty acids: 10% palmitic acid, 4% stearic acid
84% simple unsaturated fatty acids: 64% oleic acid, 20% palmitoleic acid
2% multiple unsaturated fatty acids: 2% linoleic acid
19mg vitamin E /100ml

HEALTH EVALUATION: Macadamia nut oil has a particularly high content of simple unsaturated fatty acid and it is rich in vitamin E, oleic acid and palmitoleic acid.

MACADAMIA NUT OIL IN COSMETICS: Before macadamia nut oil was introduced to the European market as a food, the cosmetics industry had already discovered the pure oil. Used in creams, it is supposed to inhibit the aging process of the skin.

IN COOKING

TASTE:

Macadamia nut oil has a uniquely sweet, nutty flavor and a deep, gold-yellow color.

USE:

Macadamia nut oil is highly suitable for salad dressings, marinades and wok dishes. You can put a few drops of macadamia nut oil on fresh figs as well. It is a pity to use the oil for frying, but a couple of tablespoons of nut oil in bread dough, cake batter or pastry provides a special flavor and makes them juicy and smooth.

PURCHASE/STORAGE:

Macadamia nut oil is available in small bottles in specialty stores or delicacy sections of well-stocked supermarkets and it is quite expensive. You should store the oil in a cool, dark place because it should not be exposed to a direct sunlight, which causes it to go bad.

COOKING TIP:

If you have 2 bunches of coriander greens, a 1/2 cup of macadamia nuts, 2 garlic cloves, 3 1/2 tablespoons of grated Parmesan cheese, and half a cup of macadamia nut oil at hand, you can make a delicious pesto. Put the first 4 ingredients into a mixer and add the oil slowly while mixing.

Macadamia nut bread

Ingredients for 2 small loaves or 1 large loaf: 3 small sachets powdered yeast • 1 cup lukewarm milk • 1 pinch salt • 2 tablespoons raw sugar • 1 teaspoon ground cinnamon • ½ teaspoon ground nutmeg • ½ teaspoon seasoning blend for baking • 2 eggs • 1 lb wheat flour • 2 tablespoons macadamia nut oil • ½ cup mixed fruit • ½ cup chopped macadamia nuts

Preparation: Put the yeast and milk in a bowl and let stand in a warm place for 10 minutes. Mix the salt, sugar and seasonings, add whipped eggs one after another. Knead the flour, oil, fruit and nuts until the dough is smooth and pliable. Put the dough into a lightly oiled bowl and roll it once to coat it with oil. Cover the bowl and set aside in a warm place for 1 hour, or until it doubles in size. Lightly oil 1 large or 2 small baking dishes. Press the dough flat, put it on a rolling board sprinkled with flour and form 1 or 2 loaves. Place in the baking dish, cover and let stand in a warm place for 20 minutes. Pour the milk on top and bake in the oven for 25 minutes at 410-428°F. Cool on an oven rack.

Frisee salad with chicken breast rolls

INGREDIENTS: 1 piece ginger • 1 bunch coriander • 6 tablespoons macadamia nut oil • 5 tablespoons currant vinegar • salt • black pepper • 1 pinch sugar • 1 small head frisée lettuce • 3½ oz field lettuce • 2 pink grapefruits • 1 lb chicken breast • 1 bunch fine parsley • 3 tablespoons hot, sweet, chili sauce • 2 tablespoons oil • 4 tablespoons macadamia nuts

PREPARATION: Peel and cut the ginger finely. Wash the coriander, drain and cut finely, putting half aside. Add the macadamia nut oil, currant vinegar, salt, pepper and sugar and mix it all together. Wash and prepare the lettuce and tear into bite-sized pieces. Peel and slice the grapefruit and cut into long pieces. Cut the chicken breast into long, thin slices. Wash the parsley, drain it and cut finely. Mix it with the remaining coriander and chili sauce. Spread the herb sauce over the chicken breast. Roll up and secure with wooden toothpicks. Heat the oil in a pan and cook the chicken rolls for about 5 minutes. Cut the chicken rolls into slices lengthwise. Chop up macadamia nuts and sprinkle over rolls.

Walnut oil

BASIC INGREDIENTS: 100% walnut oil.

ORIGIN OF THE BASIC INGREDIENTS: Walnuts originally come from Persia. They had accompanied wandering merchants on their travels to Central Asia, China, Greece, and Rome for a long time before the birth of Christ. When the Roman Empire expanded, walnuts were brought north. Walnut trees continue to grow in old gardens. Because of the effects the harsh climate has on the crop, the yields would not be high if there were larger walnut plantations established in these latitudes.

CHARACTERISTICS OF THE BASIC INGREDIENTS: A walnut tree can reach heights up to 75 feet. It can also grow as a bush. Walnut trees can live for more than 100 years. The first yield can come anytime after six to eight years of growth. Under good conditions, such as in California, every tree is capable of bearing about 4000 nuts a year. Picking walnuts starts in the middle of September and continues until November. The walnut on the tree, as you know, is coated with a thick green protective layer. The shell dries slowly on the tree and, when it becomes black and cracks, the walnuts fall to the ground. At this time, it is possible to gather them up. On walnut plantations, it is a fully automatic process. There are special machines

designed for shaking the nuts off the tree so that as many ripe walnuts fall off as possible. Afterwards, they are gathered up off of the ground by special sweepers and vacuums. Then, the protective layer is removed from the walnut and the nuts are dried. Before the oil is pressed, the meat must be broken out of its hard shell. There are also special machines for this purpose.

FROM HISTORY: The German word *walnuss* is derived from the Middle High German term *walhisch nuz*, or "romance nut." This etymology shows that walnuts were cultivated primarily in Gaul, France today. In the Middle Ages, people liked walnuts so much that the regional walnut trade became national.

Now, the world's largest walnut producing area is in California, where two thirds of the entire walnut production takes place. But it was not always as it is now.

Before WW I, France exported twice as many walnuts to the United States than were grown in California.

DIFFERENT VARIETIES: Walnut oil is usually available cold pressed. It is not refined since it would lose its natural flavor.

COMPOSITION:
8% saturated fatty acids: 5% palmitic acid, 3% stearic acid
20% unsaturated fatty acids: 20% oleic acid
72% polyunsaturated fatty acids: 60% linoleic acid, 12% linolenic acid
12mg vitamin E /100ml

HEALTH EVALUATION: Walnut oil significantly contributes to the formation of linolenic acid, which is one of the essential fatty acids. Linolenic acid is thought to help heal rheumatic arthritis. It has not been proven, but a lot of patients report that when they regularly consume products containing linolenic acid, they get relief from the pain in their joints and their ankylosis decreases.

In cooking

Taste:
Walnut oil is dark yellow and has a light, nutty taste.

Use:
Walnut oil goes well with salads, soups, and sauces, but it can also be used for sweet dishes, pastry, cream fillings, and desserts. It is very good with field lettuce and beets.

Purchase/Storage:
Walnut oil is available in the delicacy sections of large supermarkets as well as in health food shops or specialty stores that specialize in oil and vinegar. You can store walnut oil at room temperature in a dark place. It becomes rancid more quickly than other oils because of the high content of linolenic acid.

Cooking tips:
When used as a salad dressing, walnut oil goes very well with sweeter vinegars, such as fruit vinegar and Aceto Balsamico. Walnut oil should not be used for frying. If you would like to have a nutty flavor you should fry meat briefly in a mixture of walnut and soy oils.

Salad with lopinseed and avocado

Tip
Lopino is a protein product made with the seeds of sweet lupin. It is available in health food shops.

INGREDIENTS: 1 bunch watercress • 7 oz rucola • 2 ripe avocados • 2 tablespoons lemon juice • 1 small onion • 1 garlic clove • 2 ounces pine nuts • 4 tablespoons Aceto Balsamico • 5 tablespoons walnut oil • a little salt • ground black pepper • 8 oz cherry tomatoes • 8 oz lupinseed

PREPARATION: Tear the watercress and rucola off the stalks, wash, and drain well. Cut the avocados into halves lengthwise and remove the pit. Remove the pulp by cutting it out with a teaspoon and sprinkle it with lemon juice so that you do not discolor the pulp. Peel the onion and garlic and mince. Roast the pine seeds until golden brown without fat and set aside. Add the Balsamico to the walnut oil, salt, and pepper into a beater. Whip into a creamy dressing and put into a bowl. Rinse the cherry tomatoes, halve them, and add to the mix. Crumble the lupinseed with a fork and toast gently in oil. After cooling, add the rucola and watercress, toss with the dressing, and sprinkle with the roasted pine nuts.

Walnut perch filet strips on Romaine lettuce

INGREDIENTS: 4 oz Californian walnuts • 1 lb perch filet • 1 lemon • a little salt • a little pepper • 3 tablespoons flour • 1 egg • 1 head Romaine lettuce• 1 large yellow pepper • 1 orange • 3 tablespoons white wine vinegar • 6 tablespoons walnut oil• 1 pinch sugar • 1 oz margarine • 1/2 bunch lemon balm

> **Tip**
> *Serve with luke-warm ciabatta bread.*

PREPARATION: Mince half of the walnuts. Chop the remaining walnuts. Wash the perch filet, let it drain, and cut into pieces. Sprinkle with lemon juice, salt, and pepper. Roll the perch filet in the flour and then in the egg. Toss in the finely chopped walnuts. Wash and prepare the Romaine lettuce and tear it into bite-sized pieces. Wash and prepare the pepper and cut it into strips. Mix with the salad. Wash the orange and peel it with a peeler. Squeeze out the juice. Mix the orange peel, vinegar, oil, salt, pepper, and sugar to make vinaigrette. Heat the margarine. Fry the pieces of perch on both sides for 6-8 minutes. Cut the lemon balm into strips. Add the vinaigrette, chopped walnuts, and sweet melissa on top of the salad and toss. Put the salad on plates and spread the pieces of perch on the top.

Almond oil

BASIC INGREDIENTS: 100% almond oil.

ORIGIN OF THE BASIC INGREDIENTS: The almond tree originates from the east end of the Mediterranean. At present, it is also cultivated in California, southern Australia and Africa as well as in other subtropical areas.

CHARACTERISTICS OF THE BASIC INGREDIENTS: The almond tree blossoms very early in the spring, normally in February. The treetop is covered with an incalculable number of white-and-pink flowers. The leaves develop after blossoming and are elongated and oval. The fruit is apricot-sized with silky hair and green. When they mature, the outside fibrous layer cracks and the stone-hard nut with the almond falls out. The almond must be shelled. The thin brown shell around the meat is removed and the almond meat is processed into oil. Almond meat contains 64% fat.

FROM HISTORY: In the Middle Ages, almond trees played an important economic role in Pfalz and the area around Kaiserstuhl in Germany.

DIFFERENT VARIETIES: Almond oil is usually sold cold pressed. Refined oils are used mainly in the cosmetic industry.

COMPOSITION:
8% saturated fatty acids: 6% palmitic acid, 2% stearic acid
70% unsaturated fatty acids: 70% oleic acid
22% polyunsaturated fatty acids: 19% linoleic acid, 3% linolenic acid
45mg vitamin E /100ml

Did you know...?

Almond oil is made from two different types of nut: sweet almond (*Prunus amygdalus* var. *dulcis*) and bitter almond (*Prunus amygdalus* var. *amara*). The first type is used widely in cooking and baking. The bitter almond has a high content of amygdaline, a bitter substance that can release hydrocyanic acid. But it is impossible to find this substance in commercially available almond oil any more.

Health evaluation: Almond oil greatly assists in the formation of simple, unsaturated fatty acids and it is rich in vitamin E.

Almond oil in cosmetics: The oil gives flavor not only to dishes, but also to perfumes and creams. This oil is supposed to protect the skin against loss of moisture and prevent inflammation and peeling.

IN COOKING

TASTE:

Almond oil has a uniquely fine, delicious, nutty taste and a light yellow color.

USE:

Almond oil is a popular oil, particularly in Oriental cooking, and it is used mainly for desserts. But it is also perfect for salad dressings and marinades. Don't waste it by attempting to use it for frying. However, a few spoonfuls of nut oil are flavorful in dough or pastry.

PURCHASE/STORAGE:

Almond oil is only available in specialty or health food shops. It is sold only in small bottles. It is best to store the oil in a cool, dark place.

COOKING TIPS:

Mix neutral-tasting oil and almond oil in an equal ratio and fry bananas for 1 or 2 minutes. You will get a quick, delicious dessert. You can heat almond oil, even cold pressed almond oil, but you should be careful not to burn it. It is not suitable for long frying, but you can use it for brief, gentle frying without any problems.

Macaroons

Tip
*You can sprinkle
the macaroons
with powdered
sugar or a mixture
of cinnamon and
powdered sugar.*

INGREDIENTS FOR 25 MACAROONS: 2 egg whites • 7 table-spoons powdered sugar • 1 pinch salt • 1 teaspoon ground cinnamon • 2 tablespoons almond oil • 7 tablespoons ground almonds • 7 tablespoons chopped almonds

PREPARATION: Preheat the oven to a temperature of 266°F. Whip the egg whites until firm with a pinch of salt. Sift the powdered sugar and gradually add it as you whip the egg whites. Mix in the cinnamon, the almond oil and the ground and chopped almonds. Make small mounds with 2 teaspoons and put them on a baking sheet covered with baking paper. Bake on the middle rack for about 35 minutes. Let cool on a rack and pack into a box.

Salted almonds

INGREDIENTS: 7 tablespoons almonds (Spanish if possible) • almond oil • coarse salt

PREPARATION: Put the almonds into boiling water for 10-15 minutes and peel. Dry on a cooking board overnight. Heat the almond oil in a 1 in deep cast-iron pan and do not let it smoke. Fry the almonds until they are golden-brown. Remove the almonds when they are lightly browned. Let them drain on cooking paper and rub dry with a dishcloth. Sprinkle with coarse salt. You can use olive oil instead of almond oil as well.

Olive oil

BASIC INGREDIENTS: 100% olive oil.

ORIGIN OF THE BASIC INGREDIENTS: There is no doubt that the olive tree is among the oldest cultivated plants. Its origin is thought to be northern Africa, Syria or Palestine. It has been used for oil since 7000 BC. Throughout the Mediterranean region, olive oil has been the most important dietary staple for cooking, frying and baking, as well as a substitute for butter, for thousands of years.

CHARACTERISTICS OF THE BASIC INGREDIENTS: In the garden of Gethsemane in Jerusalem, there are eight olive trees under which Jesus is said to have prayed. Olive trees can reach 2000 years old. Certainly not every tree lives to such a great age, but they are undoubtedly among the hardiest trees. Olive trees can grow to 66 ft, and as they get older, their trunks get thicker and knottier. They have high, broad branches with thin, lance-shaped leathery leaves. The topside of the leaves is light green and the bottom is silvery. The olive tree has very small, white flowers. Olives ripen about 4 to 6 months after pollination. A tree bears its first fruit after 5 to 10 years. In the 15th year, the crop is usually large enough to make the harvest economically profitable. Olives are picked between October and February. Green

olives are unripe. Black olives are ripe and produce olive oil with a strong flavor. A good year is always followed by a year with a lower yield.

FROM FRUIT TO OIL: Olive oil is mostly sold cold pressed. To produce oil, olives are usually picked ripe. At that stage, the fat content varies between 15 and 30%.
Over-ripe olives provide oil and putting them into hot water or slightly warming them increases the amount of fat, but quality decreases, which is demonstrated by a higher formation of free fatty acids.

It is important that the olives are pressed quickly and not damaged. The quality of the oil can diminish if the olives come into contact with the ground too long, are not treated thoroughly or are stored too long. If the sensitive skin and flesh of an olive are damaged, the olive starts to decompose. That is why there should be no

more than one to three days between picking and pressing. An inadequate preparation of the ripe fruit or poor climate conditions causes an increase in the content of free fatty acids.

The average yield for one tree is about 44 lbs of olives, which can be made into 8 to 11 lbs olive oil.

Although new methods have recently been introduced, oil presses have been working the same way for thousands of years. The best-known method is hydraulic pressing. Fruits and seeds are pulped by heavy millstones producing a mash from the olives. The mash, which is spread on mats, is hydraulically pressed and an emulsion is made with oil.

This mixture is separated in a centrifugal machine and the oil is filtered to get rid of any pulp sediments.

Over the course of time, other pressing processes have been introduced. For example, processing oils based on differing weights of olive juices and oil followed by the centrifugation of the residuals (the Sinolea method). Another method involves using an unlimited spiral system with strong decanters that separate the oil directly from the juices in one step, usually before it is filtered. The marc is sold to enterprises that process extracts. The press temperature corresponds approximately to the temperature of the human body. The modern pressing systems have displaced the traditional hydraulic presses more and more. The main advantage of the new press generation is the fast, unrestricted production that avoids the troublesome, long storage of olives before pressing, and maintains consistently good quality. Above all, the quality of the fruit is the most important factor for high quality oil.

HISTORICALLY: The history of the olive tree dates back to classical Greece and Rome. The luxurious trading goods were not only a nutrient, but had many daily functions. The importance of the olive tree and its fruit in religious and secular life is reflected not only in written documents and art, but in the customs and holidays which show the major role played by olive oil to this day. Therefore, it is no wonder that you can find one of the oldest cultivated plants in one of the oldest books as well. In chapter 8 of the Old Testament, there is the story about Noah and how, after the flood, he sent out a dove that came back with an olive branch in its beak.

DIFFERENT VARIETIES: Most olive oils are cold pressed. There are 27 chemical parameters that are divided into quality classes. However, the critical factor for quality classification is the taste test carried out by experts.

EXTRA VIRGIN OLIVE OIL is only made by mechanical processes. The European Union has declared that the content of free fatty acids in

olive oil may be a maximum of 0.07 oz per 3½ oz of oil. Since 1 November 2003, the permissible level of free fatty acids has been decreased to 0.28 oz per 3½ oz. In color, taste and smell, the oil must be flawless. Oils are evaluated by taste tests.

ALTHOUGH VIRGIN OLIVE OIL is obtained in the same way, the permissible level of free fatty acids is higher, to be precise, a maximum of 0.07 oz per 3½ oz of oil. If there is an imperfection in the taste, it cannot be sold either. It has to be further refined, and it is marked one category lower.

Olive oil contains only refined oil. It contains free fatty acids at a maximum of 0.05 oz per 3½ oz. Since 1 November 2003, the limit of free fatty acids has been decreased to 0.03 oz per 3½ oz. In taste, these oils are rather light, which is a result of the refinement.

OLIVE OIL made from marc is produced by pressing the remaining olive oil, which is called the trester. The trester still has a high amount of residual fat, which is extracted from the marc. Olive oil made from marc contains only oil from the extraction and refinement of olive oil marc and the oil that comes from olives. The level of free fatty acids was 0.05 oz per 3½ oz oil. Since 1 November 2003, the limit has become stricter, and only 0.03 oz of fatty acid per 3½ oz of oil is allowed.

THE QUALITY CATEGORIES IN THE LANGUAGE OF INDIVIDUAL COUNTRIES:

German	Natives Olivenöl extra	Natives Olivenöl	Olivenöl	Zliventresteröl
French	Huile d'olive vierge extra	Huile d'olive vierge	Huile d'olive	Huile de grignons d'olive
English	Extra virgin olive oil	Virgin olive oil	Olive oil	Olive residue oil
Italian	Olio extra-vergine d'oliva	Olio vergine d'oliva	Olio d'oliva	Olio di sansa di oliva
Portuguese	Azeite virgem extra	Azeite virgem	Azeite	Oleo de bagaco de azeitona
Spanish	Aceite de oliva virgen extra	Aceite de oliva virgen	Aceite de oliva	Aceite de oruja de oliva

COMPOSITION:
15% saturated fatty acids: 11% palmitic acid, 4% stearic acid
74% unsaturated fatty acids: 74% oleic acid
11% polyunsaturated fatty acids: 10% linoleic acid, 1% linolenic acid
14mg vitamin E /100ml

HEALTH EVALUATION: Olive oil, along with canola oil, is among fats rich in oleic acid. Oleic acid plays a very important role in the prevention of heart and circulatory diseases. Another health benefit of olive oil, based on secondary plant substances in microcoverings, is that it helps prevent harmful processes, such as the oxidation of lipids caused by free radicals. Another beneficial substance for health is squalene. There is between 200 and 700 mg of squalene per 100g of olive oil. Epidemiological studies suggest that squalene protects against breast and pancreatic cancer.

COOKING TIP

During the grilling season, you can make a very delicious marinade from olive oil, lemon juice, garlic, rosemary, thyme and pepper. Simply let the meat sit in the marinade for a couple of hours at room temperature before grilling.

In cooking

Taste:

There is a wide variety of olive oil flavors. There are both light and heavy oils. The oil has a light green color, and, for olive oil fans, sediment is a sign of quality.

Use:

Olive oil is common in Mediterranean countries. You can use olive oil for stewing, frying and braising. The category "olive oil," a blend of refined and virgin olive oil, withstands temperatures of up to 410°F and is suitable for deep-frying as well. Many users find it wasteful to use expensive and spicy olive oil to fry. They use it only for salads, dips and cold appetizers.

Purchase/Storage:

Olive oil is available in supermarkets, health food stores and specialty stores. Generally, the oil you find in smaller stores has been produced in small mills. Dripping oil, a special, traditionally manufactured oil, is available only in specialty stores. It is recommended to store olive oil in a cool, dark place, as with any other oil. Although it condenses at 46°F (8°C), there is no quality loss since it becomes clear again at higher temperatures.

Paella Valenciana

INGREDIENTS FOR 6 PEOPLE: 4 oz cuttlefish rings • 1 onion • 2 garlic cloves • 1 pepper • 2 tomatoes • 2 chicken legs • 2 rabbit legs• salt • black pepper • 7 oz clams • 10–15 prawns in their shell • 4 tablespoons olive oil • 1 cup round grain rice • ½ cup white wine • 2 to 3 cups chicken bouillon • 1 pinch saffron fibers • 1 cup frozen peas • 7 tablespoons olives

PREPARATION: Allow the cuttlefish rings to thaw if frozen. Peel the onion and garlic and dice. Halve the pepper and cut into strips. Dice the tomatoes. Cut the chicken and rabbit legs through at the joints. Wash the meat, drain it and add salt and pepper. Wash the prawns and clams. In a paella pan, heat half of the oil. Fry the prawns and clams briefly, remove and keep warm. Heat the remaining oil in the pan. Cook the onions and garlic first, then the strips of pepper. Add, and cook briefly, the tomato. Add the rice and heat while mixing. Heat the wine and the 2 cups bouillon, melt the saffron in it. Add the bouillon to the rice, bring to the boil. Put the pieces of meat into the rice and simmer covered for 10 minutes. Add the prawns, clams and peas. Let stand covered for another 5-8 minutes. Finally, add more bouillon to taste. Season with salt and pepper to finish the dish. Garnish the paella with olives, serve in the pan.

Farmer's salad

INGREDIENTS: 5 tomatoes • 1 salad cucumber • 1 pepper • 1 onion • 1 teaspoon salt • 4 tablespoons red wine vinegar • 5-6 tablespoons olive oil • 7 oz Greek goat cheese • ground pepper • 2 tablespoons chopped oregano • ½ cup green and black olives

PREPARATION: Wash and quarter or slice the tomatoes. Wash and slice the cucumber. Halve the pepper, remove the seeds and slice. Peel onion and cut it into rings. Mix everything in a bowl. Add salt, oil and vinegar and sprinkle over the salad ingredients. Cut the goat cheese into cubes and mix in. Sprinkle with pepper and oregano and garnish with olives.

Tip
This dish goes well with un-leavened bread and strong, dark red wine.

Olive oil does not become olive oil immediately

Most consumers swear by the healthy reputation of olive oil and the extra virgin and cold pressed oils are especially popular.

The presentation of olive oil awards Each year in the spring, various national olive oil competitions are organized in European olive oil producing countries. The critical factors are the sensory qualities of olive oil: its taste and smell. Over 250 different varieties of olive trees account for the flavor diversity, which also depends on location, soil quality, climate, degree of ripeness and other factors.

Italy: Italy has the largest variety of olive trees. You can find over 100 different types in the area between Liguria and Sicily. In Liguria, the delicious, rather sweet Taggiasca olives prevail, but other types of olives such as Mortino, Razzola, Lizona and Lavagnina are grown there as well.

The same goes for the other regions. Tuscan olive oil made with Frantoio, Leccino, Moraiolo and other types have a deep green, fruity flavor. In this case, olives have been picked early. If they had been picked during the correct stages of ripening, you would get a more balanced taste with less bitterness. Experts then refer to a "sweetish" olive oil.

PORTUGAL: In Portugal, the most common types are Carrasquenha, Galega and Rendondil. They are pleasantly fruity and often have a slightly nutty flavor. Most of the regions in Portugal have a "Protected designation of origin" for their oils.

FRANCE: In the southern France, Picholine and Aglandeau olives are used to produce a very delicious, mildly sweet and light olive oil.

GREECE: Over 25 different olive varieties grow in Greece. The most well known are the Koroneiki, Kalamata and Mastoidis. Greek olive oils have a moderate, not overly fruity flavor and, depending on the region, they taste similar to bitter almonds.

SPAIN: The biggest producer of olive oil in the European Union is Spain. The regions where some types are grown are very large. In Catalonia, the Verdial de Badajoz, Empletre and Arbequinha oils are produced. The flavor is slightly sweetish, fruity with a hint of bitter almonds (Empletre).

In Andalusia there are long plantations with olives such as Picual (fruity with the flavor of black currant), Hojiblanca (fruity, slightly sweetish), Cornicabra (flavored, fruity), Lechin (stronger olive taste) and Verdial in southern Andalusia, which has a rather fruity and pleasantly sweet flavor.

"CUVEE" AND PURE OLIVE OIL: It is possible to find pure olive oils in all of the European agricultural regions mentioned above. However, there are also plantations where 2 to 4 different types of olives are grown. Their blend naturally gives a particularly pleasant fruitiness. They are pressed as soon as they are ripe. Finally, different olive oils are mixed after pressing, resulting in a consistent, varietal taste.

The different aspects and intensities of the typical olive flavor are always stressed. This is best demonstrated at a temperature between 77° and 82°F when you taste the oil with your whole mouth.

THE BEST-KNOWN TYPES OF OLIVE OIL IN THE EUROPEAN COUNTRIES:

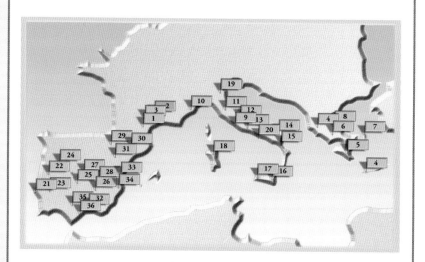

France:
1) Aglandau
2) Picholine
3) Grossane

Greece:
4) Koroneiki
5) Kalamata
6) Mastoidis
7) Adramitini
8) Chalkidiki

Italy:
9) Pendolino
10) Tagglasca
11) Leccino
12) Moraiolo
13) Frantoio
14) Coratina
15) Carolea
16) Biancolilla
17) Nocellara
18) Bosana
19) Casaliva
20) Dritta

Portugal:
21) Cardovil
22) Galega
23) Carrasquenha
24) Redondil

Spain:
25) Carresqu/Moriska

26) Picual
27) Cornicabra
28) Empeltre
29) Verdial
30) Farga
31) Arbequinha
32) Gordal/Picudo
33) Blanqueta
34) Calosina
35) Hojiblanca
36) Lechin

CERTIFIED SOURCE: Olive oils with the designation, "Protected Designation of Origin" (P.D.O.) guarantee, among other things, a consistent quality of the oil because every year the yield comes from the same limited area. It is possible, though, for the flavor to change due to the weather and the flavor is particularly dependent on the ripeness of the olives.

PROTECTED DESIGNATION OF ORIGIN: It is declared on exported products, such as olive oil, usually in the language of the producing country and it must be requested from the European commission by the producers through the appropriate national office. The P.D.O. is issued on the basis of set criteria, while the olive oil tradition also plays a role in particular regions. The producers have to describe the entire production process of the product in a process analysis (types of olives, crop conditions, storage time before pressing, pressing, etc.). An olive oil with "Protected designation of origin" must be in accordance with the process analysis and labeled correctly ("produced and bottled in ..."). The analysis challenges the producers to improve quality because each step of the production is recorded and checked. The biggest advantage of the "Protected Designation of Origin" system is in the guarantee of the source of the olive oil and of the brand name.

Origin indications for 5 European producers:

France: A.O.P. (Appellation d'Sourcee Protégée)
Greece: P.D.O. (Protected designation of origin)
Italy: D.O.P. (Denominazione d'Sourcee Protetta)
Portugal: D.O.P. (Denominaçào de Origem Protegida)
Spain: D.O.P. (Denominación de Origen Protegida)

The protected regions have very different production totals. On average, they vary anywhere between 2505 tons in Les Garrigues (Spain) to about 6.4 tons in Cilento (Italy).

In comparison to the total production of olive oil in the European Union, about 1.7 million tons, the amount of production by Protected Geographical Indications has a mere 2 to 3%.

Protected Geographical Indication (g.g.A./P.G.I.): The award P.G.I. is requested in the same way as the P.D.O. It guarantees a connection between the three production stages: the cultivation, the processing, or the production.

France: I.G.P. Indication Géographique Protégée
Greece: P.G.I. Protected Geographical Indication
Italy: I.G.P. Indicazione Geografica Protetta
Portugal: I.G.P. Indicaçào Geográfica Protegida
Spain: I.G.P. Indicación Geográfica Protegida

Palm oil

BASIC INGREDIENTS: Palm seed oil is a product made from the fruit of the oil palm and it should not be confused with palm seed fat.

ORIGIN OF THE BASIC INGREDIENTS: The oil palm has its origin in Africa and along the equator, but the plant is also widespread in Asia, especially in Malaysia and Sumatra.

CHARACTERISTICS OF THE BASIC INGREDIENTS: Oil palms can be between 80 and 100 years old. The plants are usually cultivated for 20 to 30 years because after that they are too large and it becomes difficult to pick the fruit. Oil palms are called "princesses among the palms" because they have particularly lovely leaves and a long, thin trunk. Laymen can barely distinguish them from a coconut or date palm. The first flowers are formed after about 5 years. Each flower consists of one compound spadix comprised of 1,000 to 4,000 individual florets. The fruit can be picked about 6 months after it blooms. The palms can bear up to 15 fruit pods with the heaviest ones weighing up to 33 lbs. Each fruit pod can have up to 2,000 seeds. The fruits change color from green to orange and then to yellow. An individual seed is as thick as your thumb and they have a thick husk. Their kernels consist of 55% oil which is used for making palm oil. The flesh is also processed into fat. The fat content varies from 40 to 50%.

HISTORICALLY: The Portuguese explorer Pero de Custra arrived in Sierra Leone in 1446 and he later reported that the natives produced oil from the fruit of the oil palm and used it for rubbing into the skin and as an edible fat. As early as the 19th century, palm oil was brought to Europe and the first palm fruit was transported by ship. In 1858, the first palm oil factory in Germany was founded in Hamburg-Harburg. An increasing interest in palm seeds led to a rise in the number of plantations cultivating oil palms in the colonies. Curiously, oil palms got to Asia in a roundabout way via Amsterdam. Young plants came from the botanical garden of the trading center.

DIFFERENT VARIETIES: There is no cold pressed palm oil. The fruits are gradually sterilized, cooked and the oil separated by a screw press or separators. Then, the oil is vacuum-dried so that it can be stored.

COMPOSITION:

52% saturated fatty acids: 40% palmitic acid, 12% stearic acid

38% unsaturated fatty acids: 38% oleic acid

10% polyunsaturated fatty acids: 9% linoleic acid, 1% linolenic acid;

21mg vitamin E /100ml

HEALTH EVALUATION: Palm oil contains vitamin A precursors in the form of alpha and beta-carotene. It is another plant that is repeatedly discussed in connection with cancer prophylaxis.

DO NOT CONFUSE PALM SEED FAT WITH PALM OIL

Although palm seed fat is obtained from the same plant, it is not similar to palm oil in composition. Palm seed fat has a similar profile of fatty acids to coconut fat, and like coconut fat it contains more than 85% saturated fatty acids and is solid at room temperature. Both types of fat are white, and they are used for frying and deep-frying because they contribute to the formation of saturated fatty acids. In any case, we do not recommend the use of palm seed or coconut fat in place of oil.

DID YOU KNOW ...?

As soon as palm fruit is damaged, an enzyme in the fruit is released that encourages the separation of fatty acids from glycerin. This effect is increased by high humidity and sunshine. For this reason, palm oil is extracted on the spot.

In cooking

Taste:
Palm oil has a fat flavor and an orange–yellow color.

Use:
Palm oil is suitable for deep-frying, frying, baking, stewing, braising and marinating. It is used mainly in African and Asian cooking. In Europe, it is usually processed into margarine.

Purchase/Storage:
Finding palm oil requires good luck. It is sometimes available in African grocery stores. The shelf life of the oil is approximately 1 year if sterilized and stored in a cool, dark place.

Cooking tips:
The bright orange and yellow oil should not be heated too long or at high temperatures because the valuable carotene will be damaged.

Soybean oil

BASIC INGREDIENTS: 100% soybean oil.

ORIGIN OF THE BASIC INGREDIENTS: Originally, the wild form of today's cultivated soybean came from Japan, Mandschurei, in northeastern China, and from Korea. It was introduced to Europe and America at the end of the 19th century. At present, most soybeans are grown in the United States and Brazil, not as it might be assumed in China or other parts of Asia.

CHARACTERISTICS OF THE BASIC INGREDIENTS: The soybean plant is an annual and it looks very similar to the butter-bean plant. It reaches a length of between 12 in and 6 ft. In addition to an upright variety, there are also creeping soybean plants. The plant needs only 100 days before soybeans can be harvested. Between 13 and 14 hours of sunshine a day contributes to an optimal crop. After the pollination, the seedpods are formed from relatively small white, red or white and red flowers. Each pod usually contains from 2 to 4 beans. Depending on the type, they can be large or small, round or oval. The color of the bean also varies from straw to olive-yellow, green to olive-green and from brown to black. Each bean is coated with a thin skin similar to that on green peas. The bean seed contains about 48% protein, 18%

fat, 11% usable carbohydrates, and 16% other substances. After the harvest, soybeans are dried, carefully
crushed and the oil is extracted. In addition to oil, soybeans are the basis of many foods such as tofu, soy
flour, soy sauce, and miso as well as soy cottage cheese
and soymilk.

From history: In the book, *Pen B'ao Kong Mu*, from the
year 2838 BC, the Chinese emperor Sheng-Nung described
the soybean. In China, the soybean was so highly esteemed
that it was one of five sacred plants, together with rice, millet, barley and wheat. There was a large ceremony every
spring at which occasion the emperor himself sowed these
five plants. The word soy is probably derived from the
Chinese word sou, or 'big bean.' Soybeans played an important role as a nutrient in old China. There are records
passed on from generation to generation and dating back
to the 2nd century BC informing us about the preparation
of soy sauces, milks, cheeses and cottage cheese. Soybeans
and soy germ were also included in the cuisine but there
is no ancient record concerning the use of soybean oil.

DIFFERENT VARIETIES: Soybean oil is usually refined. However, there is also cold pressed soybean oil. This variety of oil is typical for its distinctive taste and it goes particularly well with Far Eastern cuisine. It significantly contributes to the formation of lecithin.

COMPOSITION:
15% saturated fatty acids: 10% palmitic acid, 5% stearic acid
21% unsaturated fatty acids: 21% oleic acid
64% polyunsaturated fatty acids: 56% linoleic acid,
8% linolenic acid
23mg vitamin E /100ml

HEALTH EVALUATION: Soybean oil significantly contributes to the formation of linoleic acid, which is one of the essential fatty acids. Linoleic acid is able to affect the quantity of fats in blood. Soybean oil is extremely high in phosphatides, up to 3% in cold pressed oils and, in refined oils, about 0.1%. The best-known phosphatide is lecithin. It is thought to aid the recovery of the human body quickly after an injury. In addition, it is reputed to have a revitalizing effect on aging skin.

In cooking

Taste:
Soybean oil usually has a neutral flavor while cold pressed soy oil has its own unique, characteristic flavor.

Use:
Soybean oil is suitable for frying, baking, stewing, braising and marinating. It is also used more and more for dips, salad dressing or pickled vegetables.

Purchase/Storage:
Soybean oil is available in every supermarket. Dark brown glass bottles or metal canisters are more suitable for storage of the oil than transparent glass or plastic bottles. You can only buy cold pressed soybean oil in health food shops. It is recommended to store both types of oil at room temperature in a dark place.

Cooking tips:
If you like grilling lean meat and fine fish, brush it with some soybean oil before grilling. Oil forms a protective coating and the fish or meat won't dry out as quickly. It is easier to oil baking sheets and dishes thinly and evenly with soybean oil than with margarine or butter.

Pumpkin cake

INGREDIENTS FOR 1 BAKING SHEET: 1½ cups flour • 1–2 teaspoons baking powder • 4 egg yolks • 1 cup soybean oil • 1 teaspoon cinnamon • 1 cup sugar • 4 lbs pumpkin • 7 tablespoons raisins • 3½ tablespoons semolina • 1 cup chopped walnuts • 3 eggs • 1 pinch salt • 1 egg yolk for the topping • walnuts for topping

PREPARATION: Knead the flour, baking powder, egg yolks, soybean oil, cinnamon and ½ cup of sugar into smooth dough and let it stand for 30 minutes. Peel the pumpkin, remove the fibers and seeds. Cut the pulp into small pieces and braise until soft in 1 cup water for about 10 minutes.

Pour out the liquid and let the pumpkin cool. Roll ⅔ of the dough in a little flour. Oil a pan with soybean oil and spread the dough. Cover it with baking paper, weigh down the edges with baking beans, and bake in a preheated oven for 15 minutes at 392°F. Remove the paper and beans. Mix the remaining sugar, raisins, semolina, chopped walnuts, eggs and salt with the pumpkin and spread on the partially baked dough. Roll out the remaining dough, cut it into strips and put lattice like cuts on the cake. Top with the whipped yolks and walnuts. Bake for another 45 minutes at 356°F. Cut into pieces after it cools.

Blueberry muffins

INGREDIENTS FOR 16 MUFFINS: ½ cup soybean oil • 7 oz margarine • 1 cup sugar • 1 pack vanilla sugar • 4 eggs • 1 teaspoon baking powder • 1½ cup flour • 1 cup blueberries (fresh or frozen) • 32 small paper baking cups

PREPARATION: Preheat the oven to 329°F. Whip the soybean oil, margarine, sugar and vanilla sugar until foamy. Mix in the eggs. Add the baking powder mixed with the flour and make a creamy batter. Then stir in the blueberries evenly. Fill 16 doubled muffin cups with batter. Bake until golden brown on a baking sheet in the preheated oven for 20-25 minutes.

Tip
If you have a baking sheet for muffins with 12 spaces, you can bake the same amount of batter in it and use more batter per muffin.

Sunflower oil

BASIC INGREDIENTS: 100% sunflower seed oil.

ORIGIN OF THE BASIC INGREDIENTS: The sunflower originates from the area between Nebraska and northern Mexico in the United States. The area houses a lot of wild varieties. The sunflower was imported to Europe by the Spaniards. It was considered a decorative plant only for a long time. In the middle of the 19th century, sunflowers were brought to Russia. The seeds were quickly accepted by the Russian people because the taste reminded them of the arolla pine nut, which had been common fare for a long time.

CHARACTERISTICS OF THE BASIC INGREDIENTS: The sunflower plant is a composite flower. One flower can have a diameter of up to 18 in and contain about 1,000 to 1,500 seeds. Sunflower seeds are scientifically considered to be nuts since they consist of a shell and seeds. The range of shell colors varies from white to gray to black, and the stripes are black, white, and gray. Sunflowers are harvested with combine harvesters. The seeds are removed from the calyx and then dried. To obtain oil, the seeds and shells are pressed, or the seeds are peeled and the yellow or golden-colored oil is extracted.

FROM HISTORY: Sunflowers were cultivated by the aboriginal peoples of the Americas. Explorers on the American continent described how the Pueblo Indians made bread and oil from milled sunflower seeds. This oil was not only used for oiling the skin and hair, but for painting the skin in time of war. The first oil mill for sunflowers is believed to have been built in the village of Alexierka in the Ukraine in 1830. This village is lovingly called "the sunflower capital" by the Ukrainian people. The sunflower oil industry spread from the Ukraine all over southern Russia.

DIFFERENT VARIETIES: At present, the main sunflower producing regions in Europe are in France and southern

Russia. Sunflower oil is usually available refined. It is widespread not only as edible oil, but is also used in the production of margarine and mayonnaise. Cold pressed sunflower oil is a specialty.

COMPOSITION:
12% saturated fatty acids: 6% palmitic acid, 6% stearic acid
24% unsaturated fatty acids: 24% oleic acid
64% polyunsaturated fatty acids: 63% linoleic acid, 1% linolenic acid;
70mg vitamin E /100ml

HEALTH EVALUATION: Sunflower oil significantly contributes to the formation of linoleic acid, which is one of the essential fatty acids. The content of vitamin E is very high. A small serving of of sunflower oil is enough to cover the daily need of vitamin E.

DID YOU KNOW ...?

Sunflower seeds, when they are roasted, ground and fortified, serve as a substitute for coffee in time of need.

IN COOKING

TASTE:
Sunflower oil usually tastes and smells neutral.
Cold pressed sunflower oil has a mildly nutty flavor.

USE:
Refined sunflower oil is preferred for frying, baking and stewing. Thanks to its natural flavor, it can be also used in cold food to make mayonnaise and remoulade.

PURCHASE/STORAGE:
Sunflower oil is available in every supermarket. Dark brown glass bottles or metal canisters are more suitable for storage than transparent glass and plastic bottles. You can store sunflower oil at room temperature in a dark place.

COOKING TIP:
You can use sunflower oil to great effect when frying for a short amount of time. To see if the fat has the right temperature, dip a wooden stick in the oil. If small blisters are made, it is hot enough.

Steak Bacchus

Tip
*This dish goes
well with
mashed potatoes.*

INGREDIENTS: 4 thin pork steaks • a little salt • black pepper • 2 tablespoons sunflower oil • ½ lb white grapes • 2 tablespoons honey • 2 cups water• 2 tablespoons "Maggi fine onion juice"

PREPARATION: Wash the steaks, drain dry and add salt and pepper. Heat the oil in a frying pan and fry the steaks on both sides. Wash the grapes, halve them, remove the seeds, add to the fat and let heat while turning. Add the honey and let the grapes glaze. Put the steaks and the grapes on 4 plates. Pour the 2 cups of water into the frying liquid and bring to a boil. Melt the "Maggi fine onion juice" in it. Serve with the sauce.

Summer salad with pepper crackers

INGREDIENTS: 2 tablespoons butter • 2 tablespoons powdered sugar • 4 tablespoons pistachio nuts • 1 teaspoon green pepper • 1 head oak leaf lettuce• ½ lb strawberries • 1 pear • 1 pack Italian salad seasoning • 4 tablespoons sunflower oil • 1 lb chicken breast • salt • black pepper

PREPARATION: Heat the butter in a pan, add the powdered sugar and let it caramelize. Chop the pistachio nuts and add to the pan with some green pepper. Spread the caramel mash on a piece of aluminum foil, let cool and crush. Wash and prepare the oak leaf lettuce and tear it into bite-sized pieces. Wash and prepare the strawberries and halve them. Peel the pear, halve, remove the core and slice. Mix the Italian Salad seasoning with water and 3 spoonfuls of sunflower oil. Heat the remaining oil in a pan, fry the chicken breast on both sides until golden-brown and add salt and pepper. Cut in thin slices. Mix all of the ingredients and add the dressing. Serve with pepper crackers.

Linseed oil

BASIC INGREDIENTS: 100% linseed oil.

SOURCE OF BASIC INGREDIENTS: The source of flax has not been conclusively found. There are about 100 different types occurring primarily in mild and subtropical climates all over the world, particularly in the Mediterranean region and the northern hemisphere.

CHARACTERISTICS OF THE BASIC INGREDIENTS: There are two types of cultivated flax: flax used for fabrics and flax used for oil. It was the production of fabrics that was mainly responsible for flax's popularity, not the production of oil. Flax is sown in the spring and reaches a height of 20 to 24 inch. It has thin, elongated leaves. The blossom consists of five fine, light blue petals and it has a blue filament. The ovary is a pea-size capsule where there are between 6 and 10 seeds. The most important quality of oil flax, which is sorted by sifting, is that the capsules do not crack when they mature and allow the seed to germinate. Since this closed-seed flax appeared, the yields of linseed have unmistakably increased. The plant becomes more yellow-and-brown as the fruit matures. The flax is harvested and the seeds are threshed out of the capsules. The seed used for oil is

golden-yellow and not brown, as are the linseeds used for baking.

FROM HISTORY: Linseed was recorded as a nutrient for the first time by the Greeks, who ate pastry made with linseeds, sesame, poppy and honey as early as the 7th century BC. However, the plant was also known in ancient Egypt, where 4000-year-old mummies were wrapped in linen.

DIFFERENT VARIETIES: Linseed oil is sold cold pressed and refined. Because of the high linoleic acid content, it is not a good idea to heat the oil to a high temperature.

COMPOSITION:
10% saturated fatty acids: 6% palmitic acid, 4% stearic acid
18% unsaturated fatty acids: 18% oleic acid
72% polyunsaturated fatty acids: 14% linoleic acid, 58% linolenic acid
9mg vitamin E /100ml

HEALTH EVALUATION: Linseed oil has extremely high linolenic acid content. Foods rich in linolenic acid are always recommended when a person has inflammatory rheumatic diseases. Linseed oil contains more linolenic acid than most other foods and is highly recommended as a source of this important nutrient.

DID YOU KNOW ...?

The word Linseed is derived from the Celtic word lin, or 'fabric.' Its name in Latin, inim usitatissimum meaning 'very useful' or 'very necessary,' which indicates that flax was used very often and had many functions.

IN COOKING

TASTE:
Cold pressed linseed oil has a mildly sharp flavor. It is
light yellow.

USE:
Linseed oil has a prominent place in Silesian cooking.
Potatoes boiled with their skins and served with linseed
oil and cottage cheese was a commonplace dish of poor
weavers and it is regarded as a Silesian specialty today.

PURCHASE/STORAGE:
Linseed oil is usually available in health food shops. It is
recommended to store the oil at room temperature and
in a dark place. Do not buy more than half a cup of the
oil at once because it has a high content of linolenic acid
and goes bad very quickly.

COOKING TIPS:
Linseed oil should only be used for cold food or mixed
into hot or warm dishes.
If you want to use linseed oil for salad dressings, com-
bine it with sweet vinegar.
Linseed oil does not go well with mustard.

Potatoes with linseed oil and cottage cheese

Tip
You can also mix finely cut, fresh herbs into the cottage cheese instead of cumin.

INGREDIENTS: 2 lbs small potatoes boiled in their skins • salt • 1 lb low-fat cottage cheese • 4 tablespoons linseed oil • ½ cup milk • 3 tablespoons cumin

PREPARATION: Put the potatoes under running water. Place them in a pot, cover with water and add some salt. Cook for 20 minutes. Mix in the cottage cheese with linseed oil and milk. Grind the cumin in a mortar. Season the cottage cheese with cumin and salt and serve with the potatoes.

Beet risotto

INGREDIENTS: 1 onion • 2 tablespoons soybean oil • 1 cup Italian rice • 4 cups vegetable broth • 1 lb beet • 4 tablespoons chopped parsley • ½ cup sweet cream • 2 tablespoons linseed oil • salt • black pepper

PREPARATION: Peel and chop the onion. Heat the soybean oil, slightly cook the onion in it and cook the rice until it has a glazed appearance. Dilute with the vegetable broth and cook for 10 minutes. Peel the beet, grate, add to the risotto and cook for another 10-15 minutes. Mix in the cream and season with linseed oil, salt and pepper.

Potato and asparagus salad

INGREDIENTS: 2 lbs salad potatoes • 1 lb green asparagus • salt • ½ bouillon cube • 1 onion • 1 hard-boiled egg • 2 tablespoons vinegar • 2 tablespoons linseed oil • freshly ground pepper • 1 bunch parsley

PREPARATION: Wash the potatoes and boil with their skin. Wash the asparagus, remove the tough ends. Cut the asparagus into 1 in pieces, cook in 1 cup of salty water for about 10 minutes until slightly firm, remove from the water and drain. Bring the asparagus water to boiling point again, melt the bouillon cube in it and pour over the diced onion in a salad bowl. Peel the hard-boiled egg, dice and add to the onion. Mix the oil, salt and pepper to make a marinade. Pour marinade in the salad bowl and mix it all well.

Peel the boiled potatoes, cut them into not too thick slices and add them warm to the salad. Mix in washed, finely cut parsley, and asparagus.

Corn oil

BASIC INGREDIENTS: 100% corn germ oil.

ORIGIN OF THE BASIC INGREDIENTS: Wild corn, now cultivated, can be found in the area between Peru and
Mexico. The remains of wild corn were found in caves in
southern Mexico dating back to 5000 – 3400 BC. It is
probable that corn provided sustenance for primeval
man. It was also grown by native Americans. Corn spread
through Northern, Central and South America before the
European discovery of America. Columbus brought it to
Europe, where it spread during the 17th century.
Historically, countries where there has been important
corn production include Italy, the Balkan Peninsula and
Russia.

CHARACTERISTICS OF THE BASIC INGREDIENTS: Corn is an
annual cereal. Its special characteristic is monoclinic, separate dissemination. This means that there are panicles
with the male flowers on the top of the stalk. The female
flowers sprout as side outgrowths from the center of the
leaves, where later, a corncob grows. Depending on the
type of corn, one plant has between one and twelve cobs
reaching lengths between 1 to 20 in. The types of corn
now grown in the United States and Europe are artifi-
cially produced hybrids which provide a very high yield.

The cobs are threshed to release the kernels from the cobs and then dried. The kernels are left to rise in water in order to separate them from the cornstarch and corn germ. Finally, the germ is separated from the kernels with separators and special equipment.

FROM HISTORY: In the mythology of Native Americans, corn is a gift from the gods. It appeared when Hiawatha, son of the West wind, met the god Mondamin, a friend of people. An Indian legend describes how, after Mondamin was killed in a fight with Hiawatha, the body of the defeated god fertilized life-giving cornfield. Corn, known as culinary gold by the Aztecs, provided an important food source for more than a thousand years. It was milled into flour or groats and used to prepare meal and to bake the unleavened bread which is common in Mexico even today.

DIFFERENT VARIETIES: Corn oil is usually sold refined, although there is also a small market for cold pressed corn oil. Cold pressed oil differs from the refined variant in its yellow-gold and mildly reddish color and its cereal-like taste. Corn oil is often used in the production of margarine.

COMPOSITION:
15% saturated fatty acids: 10% palmitic acid, 5% stearic acid
33% simple unsaturated fatty acids: 33% oleic acid
52% multiple unsaturated fatty acids: 51% linoleic acid, 1% linoleic acid
42mg vitamin E /100ml

HEALTH EVALUATION: Corn oil assists in the formation of linoleic and oleic acid. Both acids have a positive influence on the number of lipids and the cholesterol level.

IN COOKING

TASTE:
Refined corn oil usually tastes and smells neutral.
Cold pressed oil has a distinct corn flavor.

USE:
Corn oil is suitable for frying, baking, stewing, braising and marinating. It is used for cold food to prepare dips, salad dressing or to pickle vegetables.

PURCHASE/STORAGE:
Corn oil is available in every supermarket. Dark brown glass bottles or metal canisters are more suitable for the storage of the oil than transparent glass or plastic bottles. Cold pressed corn oil is usually available in health food stores. It is recommended to store it in a dark place at room temperature.

COOKING TIPS:
Thanks to its relatively high oleic acid content and natural flavor, corn oil is suitable for frying and braising.
Corn oil can be mixed with nut oils or fruit vinegars to make salad dressings.

Corn Eintopf with chicken

INGREDIENTS: 1 small soup chicken (2 lbs) • 1 carrot
• 2 oz celery • 1 onion • 2 tablespoons corn oil
• salt • 1 bunch spring onions • 1 small piece ginger
• 2 cans corn kernels • 2 teaspoons cornstarch • 2 tablespoons lemon juice • black pepper

PREPARATION: Wash the soup chicken thoroughly. Dice
the carrot and celery. Peel the onion and dice. Heat the
corn oil and fry the cut vegetables. Boil it with about 2
cups of water and put the chicken in the boiling liquid.
Salt. Let simmer for about 40 minutes. Wash and prepare
the onions and cut them into rings. Peel the ginger and
grate finely. Remove the chicken, let it cool and skin it.
Take the meat off the bones and dice. Remove the fat
from the broth, pass through a fine sieve and pour back
into the pot. Combine half of the corn kernels with about
half a cup of bouillon in a tall bowl and blend. Bring the
bouillon to a boil, adding the blended and whole corn
kernels, chicken and onions. Mix the cornstarch with
some water. Stir it in the boiling soup and let it all boil
again. To finish, season with ginger, lemon juice, salt and
pepper.

Tortillas with pepper and corn filling

INGREDIENTS: 1 small pepper • 1 small onion • 1 teaspoon corn oil • 5 tablespoons corn (from a can) • salt • cayenne pepper • some dried thyme • 2 tortillas

PREPARATION: Wash and prepare 1 pepper and cut it into thin strips. Peel and chop the onion finely. Heat the corn oil in a pan and heat the corn in it for about 5 minutes. Let the corn drain, put it into the pan and heat briefly. Season the corn with salt, cayenne pepper and thyme. Warm the tortillas in the oven for a couple of minutes according to the instructions on the package, take them out, put the corn on the warm tortillas and roll up.

Wheatgerm oil

BASIC INGREDIENTS: 100% wheatgerm oil.

ORIGIN OF THE BASIC INGREDIENTS: Wheat was gathered
as early as 8000 years ago. As individual grains were lost
near dwellings, new wheat plants appeared there. This
could be why people started to cultivate wheat. A wild
form of modern wheat comes from the European and
Asian regions. It is difficult to determine its exact origin.

CHARACTERISTICS OF THE BASIC INGREDIENTS: Wheat is the
most important grain in western agriculture. Its ears are
not hairy, unlike other grains. The plants prefer heavy
soils that retain water very well. The crop starts in
August. The grains are dried on the plants and threshed.
Primarily, wheat is grown as a starch and is used mainly
as a grain for bread. Oil can be extracted by cold pressing or extraction from the wheatgerm that is separated
from the rest of the grain. The fat content of the wheat
grains is 2%; wheatgerms contain from 6 to 8% fat. That
means that only a small amount of oil is extracted. Nearly
one ton of wheat is needed to make two liters of oil.

FROM HISTORY: The fact that wheat has been an important
staple for thousands of years can be demonstrated by the
Sumerians, who called their first coin a "shekel". That

means wheat, and "Kel" is an old unit of measurement meaning half an acre. The coin became a symbol for a value of one "Scheffel" of wheat. It is not clear when wheatgerm oil was first used as a nutrient. In 1938, vitamin E was separated from wheat germoil for the first time. Its chemical structure could then be analyzed.

DIFFERENT VARIETIES: Wheatgerm oil is usually sold cold pressed. Due to the low fat content in wheatgerm, it is traditionally obtained by extraction. Cold pressed wheat germ oil has a high content of vitamin E along with lecithin and vitamin A.

COMPOSITION:

16% saturated fatty acids:

12% palmitic acid, 4% stearic acid

22% unsaturated fatty acids: 22% oleic acid

62% polyunsaturated fatty acids: 57% linoleic acid,

5% linolenic acid

208mg vitamin E /100ml

HEALTH EVALUATION: Wheatgerm oil has the highest content of natural vitamin E of any vegetable oil. It is used by dieticians as a supplementary oil in nutrition. That means that it is added to many products, such as jars of baby food, to optimize the vitamin E content. Vitamin E works as a natural antioxidant in the human body. Since the human body is constantly being exposed to physical as well as psychological stress, some undesired products of metabolism, such as free radicals, are formed. These are neutralized by vitamin E, which stops their harmful effects.

DID YOU KNOW ...

Wheat germ oil is a very good oil for skin care and also prevents ageing. It helps with skin problems, supports the connective tissues of the skin, and revitalizes of cells. It is good for dry and inflamed skin.

IN COOKING

TASTE:
Cold pressed wheatgerm oil has a pleasant cereal-like taste and an orange-yellow color.

USE:
Wheat germ oil does not tolerate heat, and therefore it is used mainly to prepare cold food. It goes very well with raw food, and salads. You can add it to dips or thickened soups as well.

PURCHASE/STORAGE:
Wheatgerm oil is not very cheap, and it is available in health food shops. You should consume open bottles within two months, meanwhile storing them well sealed in the refrigetator. You can keep sealed bottles for about eight months.

COOKING TIP:
One spoonful of wheatgerm oil contains a sufficient daily supply of vitamin E. You can mix the oil with sunflower or corn oil.

Green spelt soup

Tip

If you want to make soup quickly, you can use about a pound of frozen soup vegetables (not thawed) instead of fresh vegetables.

INGREDIENTS: ½ lb carrots • 2 leeks • 4 oz celeriac • 2 tablespoons sunflower oil • 3 oz green spelt groats • 1 cup vegetable broth • salt • black pepper• 4 oz sour cream • 2 tablespoons wheatgerm oil • 4 tablespoons curly parsley • 4 tablespoons chives

PREPARATION: Wash the vegetables. Prepare the carrots and cut them into slices about 1/2cm thick. Wash and prepare the leeks and cut them into rings. Peel the celeriac and dice. Heat the sunflower oil in a pot, roast the groats briefly, and then dilute with the broth. Add the diced vegetables. Bring to a boil and braise for about 20 minutes. Purée until smooth. Stir the sour cream and wheatgerm oil into the soup when it has stopped boiling, salt and pepper. Garnish with the parsley and chives.

Mushroom Carpaccio

INGREDIENTS: 2½ tablespoons pine seeds • 1 lb large mushrooms • 1–2 tablespoons balsamic vinegar • a little salt • black pepper • 5–6 tablespoons wheatgerm oil • 1 bunch basil • 2 oz Parmesan cheese

PREPARATION: Roast the pine seeds in a dry pan, take them out, and let cool. Prepare the mushrooms and wash if necessary. Cut the mushrooms into thin slices and put on 4 plates. Mix the vinegar, salt, pepper, and oil; sprinkle on the mushrooms. Wash the basil and shake dry. Tear the basil leaves into pieces. Grate the Parmesan. Sprinkle the mushrooms with the basil and Parmesan.

Tip
If you have no wheatgerm oil on hand, you can use cold pressed olive oil or canola oil.

Poppyseed oil

BASIC INGREDIENTS: 100% poppyseed oil

ORIGIN OF THE BASIC INGREDIENTS: The opium poppy is supposed to have its origin in Asia Minor and the Mediterranean. It is difficult to determine its source exactly because it was first cultivated in the early Stone Age. Now it is grown in Turkey, Greece and India.

CHARACTERISTICS OF THE BASIC INGREDIENTS: The herb-like, annual plant, which reaches a height between 28 and 47 in, has light green leaves and white, violet or reddish flowers. A walnut-size capsule, containing round poppyseeds, is formed on the blossom. Poppies are rich in linoleic acid and contain a minimal quantity of opiates, compared with the plant sap. There are three varieties of poppies grown for oil: the white poppy, also known as the Berlin poppy, with pure white or extremely red petals and white seeds, bears the seeds with the highest oil content. The closing poppy has light red flowers and blue seeds and produces a moderate amount of oil. The gray poppy, known as the pouring poppy, also has light red flowers and produces gray seeds with low oil content.

HISTORICALLY: Charlemagne ordered increased poppy cultivation on his land. At that time, the seeds were consumed directly. Knowledge of oriental cooking styles spread during the Crusades, contributing to the beginning of oil production from poppies in Germany. In the late Middle Ages, the popularity of poppyseed oil continued to spread. The plant was called "magöl," a term derived from the Old High German "mag" or "mago," meaning "garden poppy." In the Swabian dialect "Mohn" means something like "oil stomach."

DID YOU KNOW ...?

Since poppies are regulated by narcotics laws, it is only legal to grow poppies with a permit from the Federal Health Department. Poppies may be grown only when the capsules contain less than 0.01% morphine.

DIFFERENT VARIETIES: Other than Hungary, the most important European poppy producers are Austria, France, Poland, the Czech Republic and Slovakia. Usually, only cold pressed poppyseed oil is sold. No opiates can be found in poppyseed oil.

COMPOSITION:
15% saturated fatty acids: 12% palmitic acid, 3% stearic acid
16% simple unsaturated fatty acids: 16% oleic acid
69% multiple unsaturated fatty acids: 68% linoleic acid, 1% linolenic acid,
5mg vitamin E /100ml

HEALTH EVALUATION: Poppyseed oil normally has an extremely high content of linoleic acid, an essential fatty acid used in the construction of cell walls and in the synthesis of prostaglandin. Dieticians do not consider this oil particularly healthy because the ratio of linoleic and linolenic acid is not good.

IN COOKING

TASTE:
Poppyseed oil tastes fine and sharp. It is light yellow colored.

USE:
Poppyseed oil is a classic in Austrian and oriental cooking. Its special flavor seems best in sweet dishes, pastries and desserts. But crispy salads and fruit soups can also be seasoned with it. In the Orient, there are a lot of spicy dishes that include a dash of poppyseed oil.

PURCHASE/STORAGE:
Poppyseed oil is among the most expensive oils. It is available in specialty or health food shops and is sold only in small bottles at a fixed price. It is recommended to store the oil in a cool, dark place.

COOKING TIPS:
Poppyseed oil mixed with melted butter goes well with lukewarm apple strudel, donuts and crepes. Poppyseed oil and raisins are wonderful in Arabic dishes such as couscous or pilaf.

Cake with poppy crisp

Tip
*You can also
use raw sugar
or maple syrup
instead of
honey.*

INGREDIENTS FOR 1 BAKING SHEET: 1 cup butter • 4 tablespoons poppyseed oil • 1 cup sugar • 1 pack vanilla sugar • 3 eggs • 2½ cups yogurt • 2½ cups flour • 1 packet baking powder • 1 cup honey • 4 tablespoons milk • 5 tablespoons poppy seeds • 5 tablespoons sesame seeds • 7 tablespoons sunflower seeds

PREPARATION: Mix 3½ oz of butter with the poppy seed oil, sugar and vanilla sugar until creamy. Add the eggs and whip to a creamy mass. Add the yogurt and stir. Mix the flour with the baking powder and sift. Add the flour mixture to the batter. Pre-heat the oven to 356°F. Oil the baking sheet or put baking paper on it. Spread the batter on the baking sheet. Bake for about 15 minutes on the middle rack. Meanwhile, let the remaining butter melt on top. Mix the honey, milk, poppyseeds, sesame seeds and sunflower seeds into the melted butter. Let boil once again and then cool. Spread the topping evenly on the cake and bake for another 15 minutes at 320°F. Slice warm into 20 equal pieces.

Apple strudel

INGREDIENTS: 1½ cups flour • 1 pinch salt • 4 tablespoons oil • 2 tablespoons margarine • 3½ tablespoons breadcrumbs • ½ cup sugar • 2 cups apples • 3 tablespoons butter • 1 teaspoon cinnamon • 3 tablespoons chopped almonds • 5 tablespoons currants • ½ peel of half a lemon • powdered sugar • 3½ oz butter • 4 tablespoons poppy seed oil

PREPARATION: Put 1 cup flour, ½ cup lukewarm water, salt and 2 tablespoons oil into a bowl. Knead until smooth. Form a ball, oil it and let stand in a preheated bowl for half an hour. To make the filling, heat the margarine. Add breadcrumbs, fry and sprinkle with sugar. Peel and quarter apples and cut into thin slices. Coat large, smooth cloth with remaining flour. Place the dough on the cloth and roll out very thin, spreading it from the center to the sides. Preheat the oven to 350°F. Oil baking sheet with 2 tablespoons butter. Spread breadcrumb mixture, apples, cinnamon, almonds, currants and lemon peel evenly on dough. Roll up strudel and place on the baking sheet. Spread with remaining butter and bake for about 55 minutes. Remove and sprinkle with powdered sugar. Melt butter, mix with poppyseed oil and serve with lukewarm strudel.

Sesame oil

BASIC INGREDIENTS: 100% sesame seed oil.

ORIGIN OF THE BASIC INGREDIENTS: Sesame has been grown in the area between the Euphrates and the Tigris Rivers, in India and in Africa for thousands of years. Sesame spread to China, Japan and to the Mediterranean countries very early. Now, the main sesame growing regions are Turkey, India, China, Ecuador, the Honduras, Nicaragua and Mexico.

CHARACTERISTICS OF THE BASIC INGREDIENTS: The sesame plant has a long, straight stem that can reach a height of up to 6 ft with oval leaves. It has white or wine red flowers and its leaves resemble a thimble. All of the flowers of the plant blossom at the same time and not for longer than six hours. The first seeds ripen twelve weeks after sowing. They sit in elongated seed capsules, between 40 and 400 on each plant. The plant is cut and dried in bunches. The disadvantage of the sesame harvest is that not all of the plants ripen at the same time. Seed capsules open slowly during the drying process and sesame seeds fall out, a phenomenon which probably explains the exclamation from the famous fairy tale, "open sesame!"

HISTORICALLY: Sesame seed oil was sacrificed to the gods in India in the time of Altharradeda along with rice, barley and beans. In the Greek Orthodox Church, the Sanctuary Lamp has been filled with sesame seed oil for centuries. Archaeological discoveries on the islands of Crete and Kalliste in the Aegean Sea establish that sesame seed oil was used in the religious life of the ancient Greeks at births, weddings and funerals.

DID YOU KNOW …?

According to the law of 1897, sesame seed oil had to be added to margarine (10%) and to processed cheese (5%).

DIFFERENT VARIETIES: There are two varieties of sesame seed oil. Dark sesame seed oil is processed from roasted sesame seeds, and light sesame seed oil is processed from raw seeds. The latter can be further categorized as cold pressed or refined oil. Roasted sesame seed oil has a very strong sesame taste, and therefore, it should be used only in minute amounts. The high content of both antioxidants, sesamol and sesamolin, gives the oil a particularly long-life.

COMPOSITION:

13% saturated fatty acids: 8% palmitic acid, 5% stearic acid

42% unsaturated fatty acids: 42% oleic acid

45% polyunsaturated fatty acids: 44% linoleic acid, 1% linolenic acid

13mg vitamin E /100ml

HEALTH EVALUATION: Sesame seed oil is rich in unsaturated and polyunsaturated fatty acids. It has a benefit for cholesterol levels and the quantity of fat in blood. Additionally, its essential linoleic acid is indispensable for the construction of cell walls.

In cooking

Taste:

Cold pressed sesame seed oil has a pleasantly nutty taste and a light yellow color. Refined oil tastes plain and is very light colored. Roasted or dark sesame seed oil has an extremely nutty flavor.

Use:

Sesame seed oil is predominantly used in Asian and oriental cooking. Dark sesame seed oil is a seasoning for wok dishes. Sesame seed oil goes well with salads as well as sweet dishes. It is suitable for cooking too.

Purchase/Storage:

Dark sesame seed oil is available in Asian food stores or in well-stocked supermarkets. It is possible to buy cold pressed, light sesame seed oil in health food shops. Refined sesame seed oil is rather rare, but can be found in large supermarkets. Sesame seed oil has a long shelf life if it is stored well in a cool, dark place.

Cooking tips:

Dark sesame seed oil should be used with care. If you use too much oil, you will inhibit the flavor of other ingredients.

Stuffed sesame pancakes

INGREDIENTS FOR 2 PEOPLE: 1 egg • 1 tablespoon spelt whole wheat flour • 4 tablespoon low fat milk (1.5%) • 3 tablespoon mineral water • sea salt • 1 teaspoon sesame seeds • 1 small glass pickled corn kernels • half of a red pepper • 2 oz sugar beet • 5 oz cauliflower • 3 teaspoons sesame seed oil • 1 tablespoon vegetable bouillon • freshly ground pepper • sweet chili sauce

PREPARATION: Mix the egg, flour, milk, mineral water, 1 large pinch of salt and sesame seeds to make pancake batter. Cover and let proof for 10 minutes. Drain the corn kernels. Wash and prepare the pepper, sugar beet and cauliflower and cut them into small pieces. Heat 1 teaspoon of the sesame seed oil in a pot, add the vegetables, broth as well as salt and pepper. Simmer covered for about 10 minutes. Heat 1 teaspoon of olive oil in a flat pan, make 2 pancakes from the batter and cook one after the other. Spread the vegetables on the pancakes, roll them up and serve on two preheated plates with chili sauce.

Sesame crackers

INGREDIENTS FOR 1 BAKING SHEET: 4 oz spelt flakes • 4 oz fine wheat groats • 1 tablespoon sesame seed oil • 4 tablespoon sesame seeds • 1 teaspoon sea salt • 1 teaspoon neutral oil

PREPARATION: Mix the flakes and wheat groats in a bowl with 1 spoonful of sesame seed oil and about 2 cups of water to make a thick fluid batter. Let it proof for about 1 hour. Preheat the oven to 347°F. Mix the sesame and salt into the batter. Oil the baking sheet, spread the batter thinly and bake for about 15 minutes in the preheated oven. Remove from oven and press triangles or diamonds into the batter with a sharp knife. Bake for about 15-20 minutes until they are crispy. Take the crackers out of the oven, let them cool a bit and break into triangles or diamonds.

> **Tip**
> This goes well with a dip made with Gorgonzola and cottage cheeses that has been seasoned with lemon juice, salt and pepper.

Canola oil

BASIC INGREDIENTS: 100% canola oil.

ORIGIN OF THE BASIC INGREDIENTS: The origin of the canola is not clear. It is possible to find wild forms all over Europe, Asia and northern Africa. Canola might have first been cultivated in the 17th century in Normandy and southern England, arriving in Germany as early as the 18th century.

CHARACTERISTICS OF THE BASIC INGREDIENTS: Canola is sown in the fall. It produces bright yellow flowers in May of the following year. Its stalks and leaves are green and blue – the typical color of cabbage to which it is related. It loses its strong green color by harvest time in August and acquires a straw yellow, brown color. Small pods, which contain many seeds, develop, then the seed is mowed and threshed. The husk is removed from the small black and brown seeds, which are then cleaned and dried. Only the seed is suitable for human nutrition and it is processed into edible oil because it is free of erucic acid and glycosinolates. In 1551, Hieronimus Bock recorded that napa oil, made with a related plant, was used in oil lamps in the Alps. In addition to this, it was used as lubricating oil, for processing leather, kneading and for the production of soft soaps during industrialization.

COMPOSITION:

13% saturated fatty acids: 10% palmitic acid, 3% stearic acid

56% unsaturated fatty acids: 56% oleic acid

31% polyunsaturated fatty acids: 21% linoleic acid, 10% linolenic acid

30mg vitamin E /100ml

HEALTH EVALUATION: Canola oil greatly contributes to the formation of oleic acid and the essential fatty acids, linoleic and linolenic acid. The linolenic acid is the most important omega-3 fatty acid. These acids support the immune system and encourage the blood coagulation rate as well as decreasing blood fat levels.

In cooking

Taste:
Canola oil usually tastes bland and is odorless. Cold pressed canola oil has a mildly nutty flavor.

Use:
Canola oil is exceptionally suitable for frying, baking, stewing, braising and marinating. Because of its unsaturated fatty acids levels, it is also ideal for deep-frying and slow roasting. Its natural flavor enhances the flavor of other ingredients. This oil is used in cold food for dips, salad dressing or to pickle vegetables.

Purchase/Storage:
Canola oil is available in every supermarket. The light yellow oil can be stored for years if it is put into dark glass bottles or metal canisters and sealed well. Cold pressed oil lasts between six months and one year and you should store it at room temperature or in the fridge and above all, as with any other oil, in a dark place. Pressed canola oil is usually available in health food shops, organic shops or from a farmer.

Vegetable spaghetti with parsley pesto

INGREDIENTS: 4 oz parsley • 1 garlic clove • 4 tablespoon grated Swiss cheese • ½ cup cold pressed canola oil • some salt • black pepper • ½ lb carrots• 1 zucchini • 1½ lb spaghetti

PREPARATION: Wash and dry the parsley, tear off the small leaves and mince. Peel the garlic, dice and add to the parsley, Swiss cheese and canola oil. Mix and season in a food processor. Wash and prepare the carrots and zucchini and slice into thin pieces. Cook the spaghetti in salted water according to the instructions on the package. Add the vegetables and cook together for 5 minutes before the spaghetti is finished cooking. Drain, leaving about 3½ tablespoons of boiling water. Mix the wet vegetable spaghetti and pesto. If dry, mix in some boiling water.

Baked chicken legs and vegetables

INGREDIENTS: 4 chicken legs • 2–3 shoots rosemary • 3 garlic cloves • salt • pepper • sweet paprika • 3½ tablespoon canola oil • 1½ lbs potatoes • 1 lb zucchini • 1 lb carrots

PREPARATION: Wash the chicken legs and dry. Cover with 2/3 of the marinade made with rosemary, chopped garlic, salt, pepper, paprika and canola oil and stand in the fridge for 2 hours. Peel and cut the potatoes into halves or quarters and place on an oiled pan. Roast the chicken legs in a rack in the pan for about 40 minutes at 392°F. Baste the remaining marinade on the chicken legs occasionally. Wash and slice the zucchini and carrots. Add the carrots after 20 minutes, the zucchini after 30 minutes and roast to desired tenderness.

Safflower seed oil

BASIC INGREDIENTS: This type of oil consists of 100% safflower seeds and is also known as thistle seed.

ORIGIN OF THE BASIC INGREDIENTS: It is still not clear where safflower originates. On the one hand, there are some speculations that its origin is in northern India and the mountain regions of Afghanistan, but on the other hand, findings indicate it originated in Egypt and Sudan. In any case, safflower was widespread in the whole Mediterranean region by the time of the Roman Empire.

CHARACTERISTICS OF THE BASIC INGREDIENTS: Safflower is a summer plant and reaches a height of anywhere between 16 to 32 in. It looks very similar to thistle seed. The leaves are thorny and it has the deep roots typical of a steppe plant. It is a composite flower, like the sunflower. The petals are light yellow, yellow and red or saffron red. The seeds are similar to the sunflower, but they are smaller and ivory colored. Without the shell, safflower seeds contain between 25 and 37% fat. After peeling, over 50% of the oil is left. When the plant is ripe, it is harvested with combine harvesters. The seeds are then cleaned, dried, peeled and processed into oil.

FROM HISTORY: Safflower was grown specifically for its petals for a long time. They contain saffron yellow and carthamin pigments.

To obtain both colors, the calyxes were crushed, then dried or mixed with water to release the water-soluble pigment. Before aniline dyes were invented at the beginning of 20th century, this plant pigment was used for dying most materials requiring yellow, cherry red, pink, brown or yellow. Safflower yellow was also used for coloring liqueurs and the carthamin was used in cosmetics before World War I. Plant pigments have recently become popular again. The demand for products colored with safflower is increasing.

Safflower petals were sold as a false saffron as early as the Middle Ages.

DIFFERENT VARIETIES: You can buy safflower oil cold pressed, pressed, refined or even organic. The proportion of fatty acid is similar in the four alternatives. The organic product guarantees that the seeds were produced according to ecological regulations. The refined oil was produced at higher temperatures and purified more thoroughly so it contains less flavor and a smaller amount of secondary vegetable material.

COMPOSITION:
10% saturated fatty acids: 7% palmitic acid, 3% stearic acid
13% unsaturated fatty acids: 12% oleic acid, 1% palmitic acid
78% polyunsaturated fatty acids: 77% linoleic acid, 1% linolenic acid
45 mg vitamin E /100 ml

DID YOU KNOW…?

There was such a remarkable safflower trade in the region around Erfurt in the 17th century that in the year 1613 a provincial law was issued in accordance with the regulations to control it. It stated that the safflower plant was to be used first by oil traders and not as a pigment.

HEALTH EVALUATION: Safflower oil is one of the vegetable oils which are richest in linoleic acid. It was particularly recommended in the 1980s for preventing arteriosclerosis because dieticians stressed the importance of polyunsaturated fatty acids. At present, simple unsaturated fatty acids are considered valuable and safflower oil has lost its special recommendation for these fat metabolism disorders.

IN COOKING

TASTE:
Cold pressed safflower oil has a unique fruit flavor and the refined oil tastes light.

USE:
Safflower oil goes very well with salads, particularly green salads, raw fruit and vegetables and dips. You can use it for baking, stewing and frying.

PURCHASE/STORAGE:
You will find refined safflower oils in every well-stocked grocery store. Cold pressed or organic safflower oils are available in health food shops or in the organic section of large supermarkets. Safflower oil should always be stored in a dark bottle or a metal canister in a cool, dark place. Pay attention to the "best before" date.

COOKING TIP:
It is inadvisible to use safflower oil for repeated frying and baking or heating to temperatures above 350°F because undesirable and cancer-causing oxidation products, such as hydroperoxides and peroxides, can be formed even with careful handling.

Salad with sprouts

INGREDIENTS: 1 bunch radishes • 1 small zucchini • 1 fennel root • 2 spring onions • 2 oz radish sprouts • 2 oz Alfalfa sprouts • 1 tablespoon lemon juice • freshly ground pepper • 1 tablespoon white wine vinegar • 1 tablespoon vegetable broth • 1 tablespoon safflower oil • 1 small box of cress

PREPARATION: Wash, prepare and slice the radish. Wash and prepare the zucchini and cut lengthwise into thin strips. Wash and prepare the fennel and cut it lengthwise into thin strips. Wash and dice the onions. Put the vegetables into a salad bowl. Wash the radish and alfalfa sprouts thoroughly and drain. Add the vegetables. Put

lemon juice, pepper, vinegar and broth in a small bowl and mix to a smooth sauce. Add the safflower oil to the dressing. Mix the dressing with the vegetables and let the salad stand for 10 minutes. Cut the cress. Wash, drain and sprinkle the cress over the salad.

Summer salad

INGREDIENTS: 1 small head iceberg lettuce • 1 head radicchio • 1 bowl field lettuce • 1 cucumber • 2–4 vine tomatoes • 1 bunch spring onions • 1 bunch chives • 4 tablespoons sherry • 4 tablespoons vinegar • 8 tablespoons safflower oil • salt • freshly ground white pepper

PREPARATION: Wash the iceberg lettuce and field lettuce thoroughly, drain and tear into bite-sized pieces. Wash and slice the cucumber and tomatoes. Cut the spring onions into rings and mix all the dressing ingredients in a large bowl. Chop the chives finely and put them aside. Mix sherry and vinegar in a small bowl and add salt and pepper. Add more oil if needed. Pour the dressing over the salad and mix everything well. Sprinkle with chives.

Pumpkinseed oil

BASIC INGREDIENTS: 100% pumpkinseed oil.

ORIGIN OF THE BASIC INGREDIENTS: Pumpkins originated in South America and Mexico. The Spanish conquistadors who followed Columbus brought seeds back to Europe with them, where they were spread eastward to China.

CHARACTERISTICS OF THE BASIC INGREDIENTS: Pumpkins are the largest vegetables in existence. The Guinness Book of World Records notes instances of one hundred pound pumpkins. Their shoots, reaching a length of up to 33 ft, creep along the ground. The shoots are hairy and support lobate leaves. Large, yellow, funnel-shaped male or female flowers spring from their center. The pumpkin develops from ovaries, which lie between the perianth and stamen, after pollination. Botanically, it is a berry fruit, with seeds in a watery fruit covering. To obtain pumpkinseed oil, the seeds have to be scooped out of the pumpkin and cleaned and dried. Depending on the type of pumpkinseed, they are processed into oil whole or shelled. The shell of the seed contains a lot of chlorophyll and carotene and makes dark green oil.

DIFFERENT VARIETIES: Pumpkinseed oil is usually sold cold pressed. Pure refined oil is only very rarely available. Be

careful! It is possible to buy pumpkinseed oil that has been diluted with plain, refined oils. For this reason, read the label carefully.

COMPOSITION:

20% saturated fatty acids: 6% palmitic acid, 6% stearic acid

28% unsaturated fatty acids: 28% oleic acid

52% polyunsaturated fatty acids: 51% linoleic acid

1% linolenic acid

18mg vitamin E /100ml

HEALTH EVALUATION: At the age of 50, a lot of men suffer from a swollen prostate. Phytosterols, present in pumpkinseed oil, are able to prevent this condition. Pumpkinseed oil is also used in medications for irritated bladders, a typical problem among women.

DID YOU KNOW...?

Pumpkinseed oil from Styria is a specialty. Oil pumpkins (*curcubita pepo* var. *styriacae*) are planted in the spring and harvested in September and October. During these months, the pumpkin develops its mature yellow-and green color. Its skinless, dark, bulbous seeds are removed, washed and dried carefully. In traditional oil mills, often run by families, they are ground into a doughy mass. The ground seeds are warmed a little in water. Then oil is pressed, filtered and poured into bottles. It requires between 30 and 50 pumpkins to make 4 cups of pumpkinseed oil.

IN COOKING

Taste:
Pumpkinseed oil has an intensely nutty, spicy taste.

Use:
In Styria, this oil has a long tradition and if you want to cook in an authentic Styrian dish, you will want to use this oil. It is a seasoning for piquant soups and salads as well as sweet desserts. Pumpkinseed oil can be used for cooking and frying as well.

Purchase/Storage:
Pumpkinseed oil is available in well-stocked supermarkets, health food stores or delicacy shops. The oil is edible for 10 months if stored in a cool, dark place. If the oil is older, it loses its flavor and vitamins. It is best to keep open bottles in the fridge.

Cooking tip:
You can garnish pumpkin soup with a few drops of pumpkinseed oil instead of a dollop of cream. Additionally, sprinkle roasted pumpkin seeds over the soup and you will make it healthier.

Apple and sprout salad

INGREDIENTS: 2 oz pumpkin flesh • 4 oz mixed sprouts (for example: lentil, azuki, or pea pods) • 3 oz mung • bean sprouts • 5 oz field lettuce • 3 apples (5 oz) • 2–3 tablespoons apple vinegar • a little salt • ground pepper • 3 tablespoons pumpkinseed oil • 1 tablespoon sunflower oil

PREPARATION: Roast the pumpkin flesh in a pan without fat, remove and cool. Cook mixed sprouts briefly in boiling water, pour cold water over them and drain. Let the mung beans drain in a sieve. Wash and prepare the lettuce and let it drain. Wash the apples, quarter, remove the seeds and cut into slices. Put the field lettuce on a platter, arrange the apples, mixed sprouts and mungo sprouts and sprinkle with pieces of pumpkin. Season with mixed vinegar, salt and pepper. Sprinkle oil on the salad.

Pumpkinseed pesto

INGREDIENTS: 5 oz pumpkin flesh • 2 slices white bread • 3½ oz grated Parmesan cheese • 2 tablespoons lemon juice • ½ cup pumpkinseed oil

PREPARATION: Fry pieces of pumpkin in a pan without fat. Remove the crust from the white bread and cut into large pieces. Combine the pumpkin meat with the pieces of white bread, Parmesan cheese, lemon juice and oil in a tall jar and blend until you have a rough paste that you can spread.

> *Tip*
> *Spread the pumpkin pesto on freshly baked or toasted bread. It will keep in a screw top jar in the fridge for a couple of weeks.*

Pumpkin soup

INGREDIENTS: 1 lb pumpkin flesh • 2 cups milk • 1½ oz milk rice • 3½ tablespoons grated almonds • salt • 2 tablespoons rosewater • 2 tablespoons pumpkinseed oil • cinnamon • sugar

PREPARATION: Peel the pumpkin, scrape out the insides, and cut the flesh into cubes. Cook until soft in 1 cup of water for about 30 minutes. Stir while cooking. Heat the milk. Add the rice and let boil over a light heat. Mix in the almonds. Season the soup with salt, rosewater and pumpkinseed oil. Serve with cinnamon and sugar.

Grapeseed oil

BASIC INGREDIENTS: 100% grapeseed oil.

ORIGIN OF THE BASIC INGREDIENTS: Grapeseeds are found in every grape. Grapevines have been common in mild climates of the northern hemisphere, such as the Mediterranean region and the Near East and it is not exactly clear where they originated.

CHARACTERISTICS OF THE BASIC INGREDIENTS: First, grapes are picked for use in the production of wine, or must. There is residual material from the production of both these products that is called marc. Marc is produced from the seeds, stalks, pulp and peels. One option is to make alcohol from the marc. Another is to separate the seeds and let them dry before using them to make grapeseed oil. In order to produce 1 liter of this special oil, about 100 pounds of grapeseeds are needed, or approximately 1,000 pounds of grapes. The oil content in grapeseeds varies between 6 and 20%.

FROM HISTORY: Wine production must have been known to the Egyptians, Babylonians, and Indians as far back as 3500 BC. In the Middle Ages, grapeseed oil was used as a medication.

DIFFERENT VARIETIES: In addition to extracted and refined grapeseed oil, cold pressed grapeseed oil continues to spread. Cold pressed oil is rich in procyanidin, a bioflavon that belongs to a group of secondary plant material.

DID YOU KNOW …?

The production of grapeseed oil has developed steadily in the Mediterranean region and in Hungary since the 19th century. Use of grapeseeds has spread worldwide throughout every wine-producing region. Grapeseed oil is becoming more popular and is often sold directly.

Composition:
11% saturated fatty acids: 7% palmitic acid, 4% stearic acid
19% unsaturated fatty acids: 19% oleic acid
70% polyunsaturated fatty acids: 69% linoleic acid,
1% linolenic acid
15mg vitamin E /100ml

Health evaluation: Grapeseed oil has been used as a cosmetic for thousands of years. Now people know that the effect of combining vitamin E and procyanidin can clearly contribute to an improvement in the structure of the top skin layers. Small, closed wounds caused by burns or cuts heal better if they are rubbed with grapeseed oil.

In cooking

TASTE:

Grapeseed oil is green and, even when it is refined, it maintains its own distinct flavor. Cold pressed grapeseed oil is dark green and has a strong flavor. Sediments occasionally settle at the bottom, but this is not a sign of bad quality.

USE:

Grapeseed oil, whether it is pressed or refined, can be used for frying. Cold pressed grapeseed oil is preferred for use with cold food. It goes well with green salads, fresh cheese and grapes.

PURCHASE/STORAGE:

Grapeseed oil is available in the delicacy sections of larger supermarkets, in delicacy shops, or in health food shops. In wine-producing regions, there are local suppliers who often sell grapeseed oil from small oil mills. Grapeseed oil should be stored at room temperature in a dark place.

COOKING TIP:

Refined grapeseed oil goes as well with fondues as it does with beef, chicken, pork, etc. It gives the meat an enhanced flavor.

Green salad with goat cheese

Tip
This is an ideal appetizer with graham rolls

INGREDIENTS: 2 heads oak leaf lettuce • 1 bunch chives • 8 small goat cheeses • pepper • salt • 3 tablespoons sherry vinegar • 4 tablespoons grapeseed oil

PREPARATION: Wash and prepare the lettuce and tear it into small pieces. Cut half of the chives finely. Divide the goat cheese and lettuce on plates. Season the vinegar and add the grapeseed oil. Mix the cut chives into the dressing. Sprinkle the cheese and lettuce with dressing and garnish with the remaining chives.

Almond soup with grapes

INGREDIENTS: 8 oz white bread (sliced) • 4 ozroasted almonds • 2 garlic cloves • 2 teaspoons salt • 6 table-spoons grape seed oil • ½ pints water • white grapes • sherry vinegar

PREPARATION: Soak the bread in the water, squeeze, and mix with the almonds, peeled garlic, and salt. Add oil and then water. Put onto four plates, top with the grapes, and serve cold. If you like, you can sprinkle it with a few drops of sherry vinegar.

Potato salad with truffles

INGREDIENTS: ½ lb potatoes • 2 ounces black truffles • 2 tablespoons white wine vinegar • 1 teaspoon mustard • salt • pepper • 4–5 tablespoons grapeseed oil • 1/2 bunch chives

PREPARATION: Peel the potatoes, boil, slice, and let cool for a while. Mix the vinegar, mustard, salt, pepper, and oil to make a dressing. Slice the truffles over the potatoes, add the dressing carefully. Garnish with chives.

Special vegetable oils

AVOCADO OIL

Avocado pulp, which you know from the produce department, contains about 30% fat. The green oil, which is rich in unsaturated fatty acids, can be pressed from the pulp. The oil is suitable for cold or warm food. In Guatemala, the origin of the avocado plant, the oil has been used primarily for cooking by native Indians. It is used mainly in the cosmetic industry. Avocado oil mainly comes from California or other humid regions of the world.

BORAGE OIL

The borage plant is widespread throughout Europe. You can also find it growing wild on the edges of paths. The plant has little hairy, oval leaves and star-shaped, blue-violet flowers. The whole plant is edible, like cabbage, and its seeds can be pressed for borage oil. The oil is rich in vitamin E and significantly contributes to the formation of linolenic acid. It is mostly sold in pharmacies in small bottles or as capsules. Many healing properties are attributed to the oil thanks to a high content of vitamin E and omega-3 acid (linolenic acid). However, you can easily obtain the necessary supply of vitamin E and linolenic acid if you consume between 2 and 3 tablespoons of any vegetable oil daily.

Black cumin oil

The black cumin plant comes from India. It has blue flowers and forms a fruit pod with small trihedral, black seeds. Its oil is traditionally pressed from the seeds in India and in both the Near and Far East. It is extremely rich in linoleic acid. The oil is dark and has a sharp, spicy flavor. It is available in health food stores. It is inadvisible to heat it to high temperatures because it loses its flavor quickly and tastes rancid.

Buckthorn oil (wild rose oil)

The Buckthorn bush probably has its origin in Tibet. It spread from there into Mongolia and Russia. Alexander the Great brought buckthorn with him to Greece, where the plant has been used in various ways, and it is now spread throughout Europe. The plant is very inconspicuous and it predominantly grows in sandy soils on the coast of the North and Baltic Seas as well as in the gravely soils of the Alps. The thorny bush bears many berries of an orange to cherry red color. The oil can be obtained from pulp or seeds, and it is suitable for cooking. As it is extremely expensive, it is often sold in pharmacies and health food shops as a medicine.

HEMPSEED OIL

Hempseed oil has been banned in Europe because of its high content of tetrahydrocannabiol and the unregistered cultivation of the plant. At present, it is only permitted to cultivate hempseeds that are free of the drug. Hempseed oil is available in organic and health food shops. It is rich in linoleic and linolenic acid. The dark green oil is suitable for cold food, and you can combine it with other types of oil to get a milder flavor.

COTTONSEED OIL

There is evidence that the cotton plant has its origin in both the western and eastern hemispheres. People in Pakistan and India have cultivated it for thousands of years. The discoveries in ancient Inca burial sites also demonstrate that the Incas knew about cotton. Cotton grows as an annual plant, or a perennial bush, reaching a height of up to 9 feet. It has large salmon colored flowers. On the white puffs of cotton fiber, there are tiny black seeds that are a secondary product. The seeds can be used to make an oil that is rich in linoleic acid. It is not available as an oil for regular consumption, but it is used in the production of margarine.

What is a type of oil suitable for?

	Warm soups	Cold soups	Sauce/dip	Salads	Fruit salads	Bitter green salads
Safflower oil		●	●	●		
Peanut oil	●		●			
Hazelnut oil		●			●	●
Pumpkin seed oil	●	●	●	●	●	
Linseed oil			●			
Macadamia oil				●	●	
Corn oil			●	●		
Almond oil		●	●	●	●	
Poppyseed oil				●	●	
Olive oil	●	●	●	●		
Palm oil	●					
Rape oil	●		●	●	●	●
Sesame oil			●	●	●	
Soy oil	●		●	●	●	●
Sunflower oil	●					
Grapeseed oil			●	●	●	
Walnut oil	●		●	●	●	●
Wheatgerm oil	●		●	●	●	●

Raw food	Stewing	Rapid frying	Braising	Grilling	Deep-frying	Baking	Desserts	Marinating	Use of flavored oils
						●			
	●	●	●	●		●			
							●		
●	●	●					●		
●	●	●	●			●	●		
●	●	●						●	●
						●	●		
						●	●		
●	●	●	●	●	●	●		●	●
	●	●	●	●	●	●		●	
●	●	●	●	●	●	●		●	●
	●	●					●		
●	●	●	●	●		●		●	●
●	●	●	●			●		●	●
●	●	●							
●	●	●				●	●		
●	●								●

Index

A

Acetate procedure	24, 27
Aceto Balsamico	52–59 ff.
Acid-base-diet	30
Almond oil	194
Apple and lemon balm vinegar	50
Apple vinegar	101
Apple vinegar elixir	106
Aromatherapy	161
Asparagus vinegar	116
Avocado oil	286

B

Malt vinegar	70 ff.
Beet vinegar	113
Black cumin oil	287
Boerhave method	25
Borage oil	286
Buckthorn oil	287
Burns	31

C

Carrot vinegar	115, 116
Champagne vinegar	82 ff.

Cherry vinegar 96

Cherry vinegar	96
Chili oil	168
Chili-vinegar	51
Cholesterol level	156
Cold pressing	148
Combined diet	30
Copolymerized vinegars	27
Corn oil	238
Cottonseed oil	289
Cranberry vinegar	50
Cucumber vinegar	116

D

Date vinegar	96, 124
Distilled vinegar	76 ff.
Distillation of alcohol	76
Drinking vinegar	11, 133

E

Tarragon vinegar	96
Extraction	145

F

Fermentation	226

Fig vinegar   124
"Fine Herb" Oil   169
"Fine Herb" Vinegar   50
Flavored vinegar   48
Free fatty acids   153
Fring method   26
Fruit vinegar   110 ff.

G

Garlic oil   168
Garlic vinegar   51
Generator or bound
    method   24, 26
Ginger lemon
    grass oil   168
Grapeseed oil   280 ff.

H

Hazelnut oil   176 ff.
Hempseed oil   288
Herb vinegar   96
Herbal and spiced
    vinegar   96 ff.
Honey vinegar   126
Hydraulic pressing   142

J

Jasmine vinegar   96
Jerez de la Frontera   90 ff.

L

Lacto-vinegar   130
Linoleic acid   157
Linolenic acid   157
Linseed oil   232 ff.
Love vinegar   50

M

Macadamia oil   182 ff.
Malt vinegar   70 ff.
Margarine   143
Massage oil   159
Mayonnaise   164
Mead vinegar   126
Milk vinegar   130

Mint oil	169
Miscella	146
Molkosan	133

O

Oil cake	145
Oil elimination treatment	158
Oil for lovers	168
Oil miller	142
Oil pressing	141, 145
Oleic acid	156
Olive oil	139, 200 ff.
Orange, ginger vinegar	50
Organic diesel	162
Orleans-process	24

P

Palm oil	216 ff.
Peanut oil	170 ff.
Pear and cinnamon vinegar	50
Pectin layer	104
Plum vinegar	94
Poppyseed oil	250 ff.
Potato vinegar	78
"Provence" Oil	169
Pulp	146
Pumpkinseed oil	274 ff.

Pure vinegar	104
Putrefactive bacteria	49

R

Raisin vinegar	124 ff.
Canola oil	262 ff.
Refinement	146
Rice vinegar	118 ff.
Rose vinegar	96
Rancid oil	165

S

Safflower seed oil	268 ff.
Schuezenbach method	26
Sesame oil	138, 256 ff.
Sherry vinegar	90
Sinolea method	226
Solera method	92
Soybean oil	220 ff.
Submersible process	24, 27
Sulfurization	127
Sunflower oil	226 ff.
Surface method	24
Surol	21
Synthetic vinegar	27 ff.

T

Thistle seed oil	170 ff.

Tomato vinegar 116
"Toscana" Oil 168
Transformed fatty acids 153
Truffle oil 169

V

Vegetable vinegar 114 ff.
Vinegar bonbons 88, 89
Vinegar essence 22
Vinegar mother 25
Vinegar pack 33, 64
Vinegar production
    processes 23 ff.
Vinegar sprinkler 95
Vinegar tasting 98 ff.
Vineyard vinegar 68 ff.
Violet vinegar 96
Vitamin E 154, 157

W

Walnut oil 188 ff.
Wheatgerm oil 244 ff.
Whey vinegar 130 ff.
Whey vinegar elixir 133
Whiskey vinegar 78
Wild garlic vinegar 96
Wine vinegar 61 ff.

Recipes

A

Almond soup
with grapes ... 284
Apple and sprout
salad ... 278
Apple cheese salad ... 108
Apple strudel ... 255
Arabian rice ... 128
Arugula-avocado-salad ... 66

B

Baked chicken legs
and vegetables ... 267
Balsamic mushrooms ... 61
Beef with mushrooms ... 122
Beet risotto ... 236
Blueberry muffins ... 225

C

Cake with poppy crisp ... 254
Chicken in a peanut
crust ... 174
Chocolate lasagne with
Cappuccino sauce ... 101
Corn Eintopf
with chicken ... 242
Cream of asparagus soup
with hazelnut oil ... 180
Crepes with caramel
peach ... 181

F

Fine apple Jelly ... 109
Frusee salad with chicken
breast ... 187

G

Gazpacho ... 94
Green salad with
goat cheese ... 284
Green spelt soup ... 248
Ground pork and
onion loaf ... 75

L

Lemon gelatin with
mango ... 87
Lentil soup with
tomatoes and bacon ... 74

M

Macadamia nut bread ... 186
Macaroons ... 198
Mushroom Carpaccio ... 249

R

Paella Valenciana ... 208
Potato and asparagus
salad ... 237
Potato salad with
truffles ... 285

Potatoes with linseed
oil and cottage cheese 236
Pickled tomatoes 80
Pumpkin cake 224
Pumpkin soup 279
Pumpkinseed pesto 279
Raspberry salad
with veal liver 112
Rhine roast sirloin 128
Romaine salad with
mango and Mozzarella 86

S
Salad with lupin
and avocado 192
Salad with sprouts 272
Salted almonds 199
Sesame crackers 261
Spiced pickles 81
Steak Bacchus 230
Stuffed sesame
pancakes 260
Summer salad 273
Summer salad with
pepper crackers 231
Sweet and sour
chicken soup 123

T
Tortillas with pepper
and corn filling 243
Trout with meadow herbs 100
Turkey, strawberry,
arugula kebobs 67

V
Vegetable kebobs
with spicy dip 175
Vegetable spaghetti
with parsley pesto 266

W
Walnut perch filet strips
on Romaine lettuce 193
Warm salmon carpaccio
with chanterelles 60

Directory of illustrations

Cover illustrations:

Fa. Acetoria, Flein (1)

CMA, Bonn (1)

Informationsgemeinschaft Olivenöl (2)

Soja-Öl, Hamburg (2)

Roland Spohn (1)

Brigitte Sporrer and Alena Hrbkova (3)

Raimund Trapp, Essigmanufaktur Carl Weyers, Köln (1)

Vitaquell, Hamburg (1)

Contents:

Fa. Acetoria, Flein 28, 84, 147, 149, 161, 269, 273, 295

agrar-press, Nörvenich 178, 183, 195, 207, 208, 219, 220, 241, 263, 264, 281, 282

AKG, Berlin 32, 139

Arbeitskreis Erdnuss (AkE), Hamburg 177

Australian Macadamia (AHC), Hamburg 201, 202, 204, 205

British Museum, London 18

California Walnut Commission, Hamburg 275, 276, 279

Wayne Chasan 165

CMA, Bonn 71, 74, 75, 77, 163, 245, 246, 248, 249

Consorzio Aceto Balsamico tradizionale di Modena 54, 56

Fa. Heinrich Frings, Bonn 19, 20, 26

Gaia Bodes Ltd. 45

Anne Iburg 92, 102

Informationsgemeinschaft Olivenöl 12, 140, 142, 225, 226, 227, 228, 230, 233, 237, 257, 258

Fa. Kühne, Hamburg 21, 35, 40, 127, 130, 131

Landeskammer für Land- und Forstwirtschaft, Graz 189, 190

Tom Leighton, Ryland Peters & Small 37, 38, 43

Maggi Kochstudio 266, 267

Fa. Mazetti 53, 55, 60, 61

Pelikan-Apotheke, Düsseldorf 33

Picture Press Vor-und Nachsatz, 136, 137

Eberhard Schell, Gundelsheim 88, 89, 293

Soja Öl, Hamburg 167, 168, 169, 260, 261

Spanisches Generalkonsulat, Düsseldorf 120, 121, 122, 236,

Roland Spohn 171, 213, 251, 252, 279

Brigitte Sporrer and Alena Hrbkova 10, 44, 64, 65, 66, 68, 80, 87, 91, 105, 109, 112, 113, 115, 116, 124, 174, 175, 186, 199, 211, 216, 217, 223, 255

Anette Timmermann 95

Raimund Trapp, Essigmanufaktur Carl Weyers, Köln 11, 13, 25, 27, 49, 63, 270

Verband der Essig- und der Senfindustrie e.V., Bonn, Vor-und Nachsatz , 13, 14, 78, 81

Verband deutscher Sektkellereien, Wiesbaden 83

Vitaquell, Hamburg 145, 148, 151, 152, 155, 192, 196, 278, 285